Tsqelmucwílc

Tsqelmucwílc

THE KAMLOOPS INDIAN RESIDENTIAL SCHOOL—RESISTANCE AND A RECKONING

CELIA HAIG-BROWN

GARRY GOTTFRIEDSON, RANDY FRED,
AND THE KIRS SURVIVORS

ARSENAL PULP PRESS
VANCOUVER

TSQELMUCWÍLC

Royalties from the sale of this book will be distributed to the Secwépemc Museum & Heritage Park and the Indian Residential School Survivors Society.

ARSENAL PULP PRESS
Suite 202 – 211 East Georgia St.
Vancouver, BC V6A 1Z6
Canada
arsenalpulp.com

The publisher gratefully acknowledges the support of the Canada Council for the Arts and the British Columbia Arts Council for its publishing program, and the Government of Canada and the Government of British Columbia (through the Book Publishing Tax Credit Program) for its publishing activities.

Arsenal Pulp Press acknowledges the xʷməθkʷəy̓əm (Musqueam), Sḵwx̱wú7mesh (Squamish), and səl̓ilwətaʔɬ (Tsleil-Waututh) Nations, custodians of the traditional, ancestral, and unceded territories where our office is located. We pay respect to their histories, traditions, and continuous living cultures and commit to accountability, respectful relations, and friendship.

Cover and text design by Jazmin Welch
Front cover art by Tania Willard, "Free Your Mind," from the series *Crazymaking* (2006), 30″ × 22″, relief print on paper; back cover photograph by George A. Meeres, Kamloops Museum and Archives, 1987.013 006
Copy edited by Catharine Chen
Proofread by Alison Strobel
Indexed by Margaret de Boer

Printed and bound in Canada

Library and Archives Canada Cataloguing in Publication:
Title: Tsqelmucwílc : the Kamloops Indian Residential School—resistance and a reckoning /
    Celia Haig-Brown, Garry Gottfriedson, Randy Fred, and the KIRS survivors.
Other titles: Resistance and renewal
Names: Haig-Brown, Celia, 1947– author. | Gottfriedson, Garry, 1954– author. | Fred, Randy, author.
Description: Previously published under title: Resistance and renewal : surviving the Indian residential school.
Identifiers: Canadiana (print) 20220228558 | Canadiana (ebook) 20220228663 | ISBN 9781551529059 (softcover) |
    ISBN 9781551529066 (HTML)
Subjects: LCSH: Kamloops Indian Residential School. | CSH: First Nations—British Columbia—Kamloops—
    Residential schools. | CSH: First Nations—British Columbia—Kamloops—Education. | CSH: First Nations—
    Cultural assimilation—British Columbia. | CSH: First Nations—British Columbia—Social conditions.
Classification: LCC E96.6.K34 H35 2022 | DDC 371.829/97071172—dc23

To the 215 + | Le Estcwicwéẏ
and all those who did not survive.
May they live on in our hearts and minds,
and may their truths continue to teach.

CONTENTS

Tkemlúps te Secwépemc

(Kamloops Indian Band)

Dear Celia,

We the Kúkwpi7 and Council for Tkemlúps te Secwépemc are happy to support the publication of *Tsqelmucwílc: Kamloops Indian Residential School, Resistance and a Reckoning*. We are especially pleased that it includes new work by Secwépemc author Garry Gottfriedson and new cover art by Tania Willard also a member of the Secwépemc Nation. We recognize that this version builds on work done more than thirty years ago with members of our nation as they shared their stories of the school with you. We wish the world had listened then: here is the next opportunity.

The revelation of the 215 children's graves on the grounds of the former school in May of 2021 makes hearing these stories from 1988 even more important. The survivors in the book, a number of whom have passed away, were some of the first to speak out publicly about the school. In this version, new thoughts from some of the original participants and their children bring readers full circle to a renewed understanding of the strength of the Nation.

We are also supportive of this publication as it demonstrates the value of respectful relationships between the people and a researcher as one that persists over time. This book is an important contribution to the history and contemporary lives of the former students of the KIRS. We wish the authors every success.

Yours sincerely,

Tkemlúps te Secwépemc

Chief Rosanne Casimir

Councillor Marie Baptiste

Councillor Thomas Blank

Councillor Nikki Fraser

Councillor Joshua Gottfriedson

Councillor Justin Gottfriedson

Councillor Dave Manuel

Councillor Morning-Star Peters

200-330 Chief Alex Thomas Way, Kamloops BC V2H 1H1
Phone: 250-828-9700 Fax: 250-372-8833
www.tkemlups.ca

Acknowledgments

2022

My good friend Randy Fred, Nuu-Chah-Nulth Nation and Elder in Residence at Vancouver Island University, provided the impetus that encouraged me to even consider this reimagined book. I raise my hands in endless gratitude to him for his provocative demands and for his unrelenting support for the work over the years. I thank the members of the Secwépemc, Nlaka'pamux, St'at'imc, and Tsilhqut'in Nations who, as co-authors, collaborators, and teachers, continue to generously tell their truths and guide me in this work: Julie Antoine, Beverly Bob, Shawn Bob, Garry Gottfriedson, Gayle Gottfriedson, Jackie Jones, Charlotte Manuel, Vicki Manuel, Annie Michel, Ashley Michel, Paul and Kathy Michel, Maria Myers, Tania Willard, Archie Williams, and the many others who spent time with me discussing the work even as they chose not to be named. I thank the Kúkwpi7 and Council for Tk'emlúps te Secwépemc, who took time from their demanding work to review the proposal and send a letter of support for the book. Special thanks to Brian Lam, publisher extraordinaire, who without hesitation saw the value of this work. And thanks to designer Jazmin Welch, editor Catharine Chen, and publicity manager Cynara Geissler of Arsenal Pulp Press, who addressed all those details to make a beautiful book out of the bits and pieces gathered.

Thank you, Jaimie Fedorak, archivist for the Kamloops Museum and Archives, who gave so freely of her time in guiding me through file drawers and personal photograph albums to many of the images included in the book. Thanks to Heather Bergen for her insightful comment on the study notes. And thanks to meticulous proofreader Alison Strobel and acclaimed indexer Margaret de Boer for the final touches. Finally, love and thanks to Didi Khayatt, who has engaged in endless conversations about this work, providing insights, edits, and infinite patience with my struggles.

1988

The author-quiltmaker thanks those members of the Shuswap, Thompson, Lillooet, and Chilcotin Nations who shared so freely in allowing her to listen to the stories. Thanks are also due to the Secwepemc Cultural Education Society Board and staff, particularly Rita Jack and Robert Matthew for their guidance, suggestions, and trust.

I am grateful to my brother, Alan Haig-Brown, for his support; to my advisor, Dr. Jane Gaskell, for her confidence and her discerning comments; and to the members of my committee, Jo-ann Archibald and Dr. Art More, for their most helpful suggestions. Thanks to Randy Fred, my publisher, for his patience and encouragement; and to my sister, Valerie Haig-Brown, and Bill Maciejko for their editorial comments. Special thanks to UBC's Ts"Kel and Education Studies 479 students and Elaine Herbert for their critical discussion.

Because of the sensitive aspects of the work that follows, contact information for the 24 Hour Crisis Line for Indian Residential School Survivors and Family is available here.

PHONE: 1-800-721-0066

EMAIL: reception@irsss.ca

MORE INFORMATION CAN BE FOUND HERE: https://www.irsss.ca/faqs/how-do-i-reach-the-24-hour-crisis-line

List of Contributors

ORIGINAL CONTRIBUTORS

ORIGINAL PSEUDONYM	NAME	DATES	ATTENDANCE	NATION
Cecilia	Minnie Dick	1900–1987	1907–1908	Secwépemc
Sophie		1918–2007	1926–1934	Secwépemc
Martha	Mildred Gottfriedson	1918–1989	1927–1930	Secwépemc
Leo		1924–1999	1930–1940	Secwépemc
Josephine		1925–2022	1935–1944	Secwépemc
Charlie	Joe Stanley Michel	1929–2009	1938–1950	Secwépemc
Mary	Anna Michel	b. 1931	1940–1951	Secwépemc
Anne	Charlotte Manuel	b. 1942	1959	Secwépemc
Neil	Archie Williams	b. 1944	1952–1959	Secwépemc
Sam		b. 1947	1952–1960	Secwépemc
Linda	Julie Antoine	b. 1948	1953–1962	St'at'imc
Alice	Beverly Bob	b. 1949	1957–1963	Nlaka'pamux
Nancy	Maria Myers	b. 1957	1965–1966	Tsilhqut'in

CONTRIBUTORS TO *TSQELMUCWÍLC*

NAME	RELATIONSHIP TO ORIGINAL PARTICIPANTS
Jacqueline Jones and relatives	granddaughter of Minnie Dick
Garry Gottfriedson	son of Mildred Gottfriedson
Dr. Kathryn Michel and Paul Michel	children of Joe and Anna Michel
Julie Antoine	original participant
Maria Myers	original participant
Charlotte Manuel	original participant
Vicki Manuel	daughter of Charlotte Manuel
Ashley Michel	granddaughter of Charlotte Manuel

Students and staff of Kamloops Indian Residential School, June 22, 1941. | *George A. Meeres, Kamloops Museum and Archives, 1987.013 006*

Prologue by Garry Gottfriedson

KIRS CURRICULUM

teach the child
domestic skills

like how to hate
the opposite sex

like pruning a tree
to blossom dysfunction

like planting a seed
to sprout self-loathing

like learning the word of God
on bent knees pleasing a priest

like discovering death 215 times
multiplied infinitely

—GARRY GOTTFRIEDSON

The Kamloops Indian Residential School (KIRS) is a stark example of the doctrine of genocide designed and implemented by the church and state in Canada. There are some who may argue that "genocide" is too harsh a word. But how else can the deliberate starvation and decimation of a race be described? Canada and the church's policy to literally starve First Nations people across this land had excruciating effects—starvation for self-sustainability through killing off the buffalo, starvation for culture and language, and starvation for love and intimacy. Every aspect of Canada's imperial rule centred on the complete annihilation of the First Peoples in what is now called Canada. Every policy was meticulously written to support genocide. These include Canadian and church policies meant to destroy natural food sources that many First Nations people depended on, to steal children, to wipe the "Indian" out of them through residential schools. Every child that entered those schools was starved for their mother's arms, starved for hearing a grandmother's story, starved for tasting traditional foods, and starved for feeling the words of their own languages on their tongues. Starvation—physical and cultural—was the Canadian desire.

In 1988 when Celia Haig-Brown wrote *Resistance and Renewal: Surviving the Indian Residential School*, it was a clear examination of survival. Her goal was simply to have Indigenous people tell their experiences in their own words. She writes, "I am non-Indigenous, I am a white woman. I think it's important that we know these stories, but I also think it's really important to hear what Indigenous people have to say themselves, and particularly at this time." As a young graduate student back then, Haig-Brown couldn't have forecasted the importance and impact of her work. Since the first publication of *Resistance and Renewal*, many First Nations, Métis, and Inuit people have written first-hand experiences of their own. Regardless, Haig-Brown's work stands as a blatant reminder that Canada's genocidal policies have failed. From "resistance and renewal" arises "tsqelmucwílc" (pronounced cha-CAL-mux-weel; we return to being human). It is evident in the stories told in this book and in the many Indigenous voices that have arisen since then.

Despite all odds, First Nations across this country held on to enough knowledge, language, and spirit to arise out of the residential school abyss. Their survival technique was to refuse to succumb to the federal government and the church's continued oppressive tactics. Indigenous people sought creative ways to resist. For example, they resisted by remembering words from their languages, or secretly whispering phrases to each other, or dreaming of songs and dances. Some survivors became "ideal" students, and some held cultural knowledge and language deep within their souls, but in the case of KIRS survivors, most never forgot that they were Secwépemc.

It is true and common knowledge that the impacts of the residential schools severely devastated the core of Secwépemc society, culture, language, and beliefs. Today, nearly 95 percent of Secwépemc cannot speak Secwepemctsín; only about 10 percent of Secwépemc have a post-secondary education; many Secwépemc have been affected by alcohol and drugs, causing dysfunctional family units; Secwépemc governments staunchly follow colonial mechanisms; and lateral violence has become a "norm" within Secwépemc society. Many Secwépemc left their home communities to find a better life. Some have returned, but others haven't.

However, the very few Secwépemc who held on to language and identity have helped and are helping to effect a tremendous change within Secwépemc society today. These people are instilling the belief that tsqelmucwílc is possible.

Since the '80s, many Secwépemc have begun to focus on language revitalization. At the same time that the original version of this book was being written, Secwépemc women were doing the work of renewal and resistance. Dr. Janice Dick-Billy and Dr. Kathryn Michel are examples of Secwépemc women who wanted to return to the Secwépemc ways. They understood that their goal would have to be achieved through language revitalization. Their creation, Chief Atahm School, was one of the first Secwépemc immersion schools to rise out of the residential school abyss. This school is still in full operation today, and it has sustained the belief that language and identity are intrinsic parts of culture. Many more Secwépemc communities are focusing on language revitalization to embody tsqelmucwílc.

At this point, I want to draw on another significant Secwépemc woman who had a strong influence on Secwépemc culture through song and dance. Her work is another example of resistance, renewal, and tsqelmucwílc. This is the late Mildred Gottfriedson, my mother. Her story is included in Haig-Brown's book, as well. Even though not much is written about her, the work she did had tremendous and powerful impacts across Canada. Mildred attended KIRS, but even so, she never forgot her roots. In the early 1940s, she began to learn Secwépemc songs and dances from members of the Tk'emlúps te Secwépemc Band who still remembered songs and dances from previous decades. Throughout the '40s and '50s, she teamed up with Joe and Victor Fraser, Adam Bennett, and later, Nels Mitchel to teach Secwépemc song and dance to their families. In the late 1950s, they created the Paul Creek Tribal Dancers. Considering Canadian policy in that era, her enrichment of this part of Secwépemc culture addressed a travesty of Canadian policy that had forbidden Indigenous dancing. Those dances remain unchanged to this very day and have become an ongoing part of Secwépemc education.

Garry Gottfriedson dancing, with his mother, Mildred, looking on. | *Kamloops Museum and Archives, Jack Kelly fonds, News Photos file 10–Indians, Photo #1970.073.010 015*

Mildred and her husband, Gus Gottfriedson, were also politically astute activists who challenged the government and the church. They were key figures who fought relentlessly for public education for their children and for all First Nations across Canada. They realized that obtaining an equal public education was critical for tsqelmucwílc. I am proud to say that Gus and Mildred Gottfriedson were my parents.

This brings me to my story as a day scholar at KIRS.

There are many parts of my experience at KIRS that I have blocked out. Some things I remember vividly, others are blurs, and much of it I cannot openly talk about nor even write about. I witnessed sexual, physical, emotional, intellectual, and spiritual abuse, on every level, at KIRS. I attended KIRS for five years, starting in the late '50s, from kindergarten until grade 4, when my parents took us out of there and placed us in public school.

My first memory of KIRS was learning, upon entering, the rule that there was to be no interaction or contact with the opposite sex. This included my sisters. It was confusing for me, especially since my older sister Violet was like a second mom to me. I was born the eleventh into a family of thirteen, and the older siblings were expected to help with the younger ones. Needless to say, my love for my older sisters was strong. This rule was the beginning of an indoctrination that affected me my entire life. Simply, the nuns, brothers, and priests indoctrinated us to believe that love was a dirty thing.

Along with this, we were taught farming skills at a young age. In line with the Canadian policy, there was very little concentration on academics. Again, this had a major impact on me throughout my school years. I had no foundation in academics and thus, when I entered public school, I was severely challenged. In addition, this made me think that I was just another stupid Indian. I hated school. I tried everything to get kicked out, from fighting to skipping classes, every chance I got. This pattern continued until grade 10, when I met an English teacher who changed my view of learning. It was at this time that I actually learned to read and write. From that point on, I had the power of words. And there was no turning back.

I cannot claim that my experience represents that of other students who attended KIRS. Sadly, some did not survive because of suicide, drugs and alcohol, total removal from community through adoption or other means, or other reasons too numerous to cover in such a small space. Still, we must remind ourselves that the experiences of First Nations students who attended this school are webbed with every kind of abuse imaginable, and the impact is intergenerational. Only in the past couple of decades have we begun to see tsqelmucwílc strongly visible and continuing to rise due to the immense efforts of those who fought for and encouraged us through higher education, healing programs, returning to our language and culture, and most important, teaching us that we are part of the land, and the land is there with us.

It is critical, therefore, to pay homage to and honour all students lost to genocide from attending KIRS, and it is critical to honour those who survived. This book does just that. It honours those who have survived. It is testimony to the strength of individuals, families, and communities forced to endure cultural genocide. It gives courageous voice to those who've shared their stories in this book, despite their fear. It was previous survivors like my mom and dad, Dr. Janice Dick-Billy, and others who set the path for survival. This book truly pays tribute to survivors; it has contributed to setting me and all of the rest of us who attended KIRS on a path toward becoming human again—tsqelmucwílc!

Foreword by Randy Fred

THE ROAD TOWARD TRUTH
AND RECONCILIATION

The road leading to truth and reconciliation for Indigenous people in Canada has been a long and difficult struggle. Much good and much bad has happened since *Resistance and Renewal*, the original book which *Tsqelmucwílc* is based on, was published in 1988.

In 1990, Phil Fontaine, the National Chief of the Assembly of First Nations, disclosed publicly in a television interview that he had been sexually abused in a residential school in Manitoba. This was a bold and unprecedented statement by an Indigenous political leader, and it served to bring the issue of abuse in residential schools to the forefront.

A year later, the Royal Commission on Aboriginal Peoples was convened, resulting in a five-volume, four-thousand-page report released in 1996 whose recommendations proposed massive changes to the relationship between Indigenous and non-Indigenous people and to how Indigenous people can and should be treated by the government of Canada. In many ways, the report is like an encyclopedia of Canada's Indigenous history, documenting many critical issues affecting Indigenous people that were considered taboo in those days, such as the sexual and physical abuse and death of children in residential schools. I had the opportunity to listen to the report being read aloud on the Vancouver radio network Aboriginal Voices. Unfortunately, this massive document did not have the impact it deserved, perhaps due to its sheer size.

Around this same time, the public reckoning of residential school abuse became personal to me. Criminal charges were laid against Arthur Henry Plint, a notorious pedophile who had been the dormitory supervisor at the Alberni Indian Residential School between 1948 and 1968, during which time I was a student. Plint was sentenced to eleven years in prison for eighteen counts of indecent assault. In his judgment, Justice Hogarth of the British Columbia Supreme Court stated, "So far as the victims of the accused in this matter are concerned, the Indian Residential School System was nothing but a form of institutionalized pedophilia, and the accused, so far as they are concerned, being children at the time, was a sexual terrorist." A second criminal trial was launched, which I attended, and I had the pleasure of watching Plint sentenced to a concurrent eleven years.

It didn't end there. In 1998, twenty-eight men, all former students at the Alberni Indian Residential School, including myself, sued the Canadian Department of Indian Affairs and the United Church of Canada for the sexual abuse we suffered at the school. (The original filing included Plint, but the court dropped him from the case because he was elderly and had no assets.)

The trial started at the British Columbia Supreme Court in Vancouver, where former Alberni students testified about the abuse they suffered; testimonies continued in Nanaimo, on Vancouver Island. The court then agreed to move the lawyers' final arguments to Prince Rupert on the north coast, as many of the former students and plaintiffs were from that region.

It was agreed among us that it was critical for as many plaintiffs and supporters as possible to show up in court in Prince Rupert. Mary Durocher, the sister of one of the plaintiffs, and others were tireless in raising money for plaintiffs and supporters to attend the trial, but it wasn't enough. Time was getting short, so five of us headed east to Toronto, Ottawa, and Montreal to publicize our court case and raise money.

In gatherings in each city, many survivors disclosed their Indian residential school experiences publicly for the first time. The stories we heard were so horrific that it became obvious that many deaths had taken place in the schools. The one story that still bothers me today was from a woman who, on her first day at school, was forced to bury a fetus aborted from a nun, a staff person in that school.

We were fortunate to connect with a consultant with the Department of Health, who helped ensure we had sufficient funds to transport a number of plaintiffs and supporters from Vancouver to Prince Rupert, as well as to house and feed more than fifty people for one week. He also provided money for professional counsellors to be on hand.

The City of Prince Rupert donated the use of the community centre for three nights in row. The Gitksan and Tsimshian Nations hosted the first night, the Nisga'a the second, and the Haida Gwaii the third. The feasts each night were amazing, as was the dancing and singing. During these evenings, there were many more first-time disclosures of abuse.

The trial lasted three days. Each morning, we walked through the city and into the courthouse, drumming and singing. It sounded awesome. The passionate display of support seemed to have an impact on the court; it was ruled that both the government and the church were liable for the abuse that occurred in the Alberni Indian Residential School.

The first part of the penalty phase of the trial took place in Vancouver, where the plaintiffs had the opportunity to tell their stories of abuse on the witness stand. This is where the Canadian justice system got ugly. The legal team representing the government and the church was adamant in painting us, the plaintiffs, as liars. The plaintiffs were not allowed to sue for anything other than sexual abuse; alternative dispute resolutions programs that came later compensated survivors for emotional and physical abuse.

Some of us also wanted to mention Mitchell Joseph, a boy who had disappeared from the school, never to be seen again. But when we brought this to the attention of our lawyers, we were told not to mention him, as it would be tantamount to an accusation of murder.

After nearly all twenty-eight plaintiffs shared their stories, the United Church of Canada finally issued a formal apology to us. Then, during private sessions, negotiations for settlements with each plaintiff began.

I felt especially bad for my fellow plaintiffs Ralph Johnson and Dennis Stewart, who were unable to verbalize the extent of the abuse they suffered, so great was their trauma. As a result, they were offered nothing by the court.

In the end I rejected their settlement offer and decided to pursue further legal action myself. The process in the court system took more than two years, which were brutal. I spent many days on the witness stand telling my story over and over. Ultimately I was awarded a measly $97,000, half of which went to my lawyers.

The majority of those who were compensated after our trial did not have to pay their legal fees, but some did, including me. It made us feel like we were being penalized for going to court. The several attempts to have this rectified over the past twenty-five years have not been successful. But I don't have any regrets, as the church and the government were found legally responsible for the harm that was done to me and other survivors.

The Truth and Reconciliation Commission, launched by the federal government in 2008 to address the destructive impact of Indian residential schools on Indigenous people, was an important stepping stone in officially recognizing the harms committed in the past from which survivors are still suffering. The commission concluded with ninety-four "calls to action" released in 2015 that provide a meaningful blueprint for reconciliation between Canadians and Indigenous people.

I like to believe that our testimony in telling the stories of what happened to us at the Alberni Indian Residential School played an important role in revealing the widespread physical, sexual, and psychological abuse of children that occurred in residential schools and elsewhere.

The schools were worse than maximum-security prisons. The abuse was pervasive, as the abused became abusers themselves. Older boys preyed on younger ones. I was raped by many older boys. Some of them became chiefs in their nations. This continues to put me in uncomfortable situations to this day.

Sadly, many of us still suffer from the sexual trauma we experienced. But more and more cases of sexual abuse are being exposed across many sectors of society. It is rampant, more so than anyone is willing to admit.

The circle must be broken, and it will be.

This nightmarish experience that has lasted for most of my life-time has, if anything, taught me the value of stories. As I listened to audio of myself on the witness stand, I realized that sharing my truth has ultimately had a positive impact on my life.

I now dedicate the remainder of my life to the sharing of stories—my own and those of other survivors.

Preface

WHY THIS BOOK?

The pain of Indian residential schools continues for so many of the survivors and on down the generations. With each telling and retelling of the stories, with each expression of horror by those who come to know, with each small effort at reconciling, the hurt is resurrected. You, who read, and I, who have written, bear witness and honour those who have spoken. And now that we have heard the stories, we have the responsibility to act and to contribute to just and respectful change.

My continuing naïveté—arising, I suppose, from white Anglo privilege—led me to believe that the work for this book would be different from the conversations the original participants had with me more than thirty years ago. I thought it would somehow be easier, that time would have brought some semblance of healing for those who experienced and suffered the inhumanity of the schools. How wrong I was.

The 215 buried in unmarked graves on the grounds of the former Kamloops Indian Residential School (KIRS) are a testament to the ongoing horrors. One more time, former students wept as memories flooded back. In messages to me, they wrote in graphic detail of blood and disease and abuse. In May of 2021, non-Indigenous

Canadians also wept, realizing perhaps for the first time how we are implicated in the horror. Those graves also refocused media and others on the original text embedded and somewhat revised here. Suddenly, this old work had new currency. First the media got in touch with me—most often looking for advice, not comment from a white woman—and then colleagues who had previously disregarded the work shifted to a new level of recognition.

Resistance and Renewal author Celia Haig-Brown at the book launch in Kamloops, 1988.

Through it all and over the years, Nuu-Chah-Nulth Elder and former Indian residential school student Randy Fred, the person who published and created the oft-cited, gut-wrenching foreword to the first edition, remained committed to the book. It was he who persuaded me, who insisted, actually, that we revisit the work. And publisher Brian Lam immediately supported Randy's wish. I had felt a strong reluctance to reissue what may appear to be the work of a white author when there are so many powerful Indigenous works available. But then, acknowledging that Randy's work was integral to the book's relevance and that the stories at the heart of the book are the direct words of the First Nations participants who had trusted me to get them out into the world, I finally heard Randy's directive. I returned to words the late Neskonlith Elder Mary Thomas once said to me: "Once you have heard the stories, it is your responsibility to pass them on." This is not my book; it belongs to the people who shared their lives with me. I reached out and rekindled relationships with the people I had interviewed and the children and grandchildren of those who had passed on, and we circled back to meanings and emotions that lay within their words. Herein lies a slightly revised original text nested and encircled by contributions from some of the original participants and their descendants, who continue to work through the impacts of Indian residential school down the generations.

As I connected once more with the people involved, their responses to my invitation to contribute to the new edition of the book were heartfelt—in the strongest sense of the word—and moving. For some, reawakening the agony was too much; revisiting it was not an option. Their way to cope with the horrors has been to move on and away from the stories. For others, the opportunity to revisit was welcome, even while it was overwhelmingly painful. Some embraced the idea of replacing the pseudonyms in the original version with their real names or their parents' real names. Others preferred to stay anonymous, perhaps to numb the sorrow and controversy that can arise within families. Still others are writing their own stories and want to keep their focus there. And some insist that the impact is and has been manageable as they have moved through their lives.

In October 2021, before I had even been asked to think about a new edition, two unexpected messages brought me back to the work. Although I had maintained relationships with most of the people I interviewed and/or their family members, I had lost touch with two of them. That fall, in separate messages from different locations, their children reached out to me, independently and unprompted. One was reading *Resistance and Renewal* for a course, and the other sent a video message via Facebook Messenger. With permission, I share part of one of those messages here. I had first met Shawn when she was ten and her mom was a student in the Native Indian Teacher Education Program.

> Hi Celia, it's Shawn. Beverly Bob is my mum and she's upstairs, and I just thought I'd drop you a quick line. Thank you again for bringing forward the truth and thank you again for all the hard work and dedication, perseverance you put into it. I think of how you and Mum were the trailblazers for the truth—truth tellers—that's how I tell it, anyways. She helped other survivors by hearing their lived experiences. It took a toll for sure. But she did this with so much grace and dignity. She holds a standard of humanitarianism that helps us maintain clarity and insight. Mum's doing good and hope we can have a visit sometime soon. Take care.[1]

---

1 Shawn Bob, Facebook Messenger message to author, October 9, 2021.

Since that time, Bev, Shawn, the others, and I have caught up on each other's lives through Zoom and email and phone calls—relationships new and renewed. Serendipity? Uh-huh. The spirit guides us.

All of this is to say that there is nothing easy about this work, especially for the people who have taken the time to speak with me. There is nothing easy in any aspect of Indian residential schools, no matter how much time has passed. We could say that it is part of history that will always leave us inconsolable. There are those who have survived by focusing only on a few positive experiences; there are those who have survived by moving on and refusing to engage with the stories; there are those who have survived by holding tightly to what they were taught before the residential schools. And there are those who are willing to come full circle, to come back once more to the stories, back to the experiences, as a way for their truths as human beings to finally be heard and, perhaps, to influence real change. For some the return simply allows them to put one foot in front of the other and keep moving through their days.

LOOKING BACK TO LOOK FORWARD

The original book was based on my master's thesis. It was the first piece of extensive writing I had ever done, and it came well before the class action suit that led to the Indian Residential Schools Settlement Agreement[2] and also well before the Truth and Reconciliation Commission's extensive work.[3]

2 See the Indian Residential Schools Settlement Agreement at https://www.residentialschoolsettle ment.ca/IRS%20Settlement%20Agreement-%20ENGLISH.pdf.

3 See the National Centre for Truth and Reconciliation's full list of reports and updates at https:// nctr.ca/records/reports/#nctr-reports.

Looking back at the original work now, I see places where I wish that I had been stronger in my choice of words regarding what the survivors said and my analysis of where responsibility for action lies. My colleague, Anishinaabekwe Kaaren Dannenmann, brought such clarity to the way that residential schools contributed to removing First Nations peoples from their lands, their kinship with those lands, and their traditional knowledges. Contemporary Land Back movements, which focus on reclaiming stewardship in relation to traditional lands, are based firmly in this understanding.[4] Responsibility for what happened lies with all of Canada and all Canadians, both in the time of residential schools and in the present. The government and the churches worked hand in hand to enact cultural genocide. While academics and the Canadian government were and still are questioning and rejecting the word "genocide," Randy Fred not only named "cultural genocide" in his original foreword, he also detailed its stages and forms as related to the schools. Simply forgetting this history does not erase it—there are debts to be paid. We all should know the stories by now. What are we going to do about them?

Revisiting the text with what I know now, I have made some small changes and inserted new and different starting points for some conversations. One thing I have never been able to achieve, no matter how many Indigenous people have tried to educate me, is properly articulating the humour and the joy that can be integral to survival, to withstanding pain. Even through the pain that has come up again in recent conversations with survivors, laughter and love find their way in. I see places where, as a then very new academic, I was nodding in the direction of objectivity on a topic that affected me emotionally, intellectually, and spiritually—the stories that my

4 See, for example, 4Rs Youth Movement at https://4rsyouth.ca/land-back-what-do-we-mean/.

friends and relatives had been telling me for years. Such stories can never sink to being mere objects; they hold powerful truths and calls to action for those who take the time to listen.

Of course, times have changed, along with many shifts in the willingness of Canadians to recognize and accept Indigenous people's presence in and claim to these lands now called Canada. Simple word changes push complex and developing understandings to the fore. "Indian," "Native," "Shuswap," "Thompson," "Lillooet," and "Chilcotin" are all words that appeared in the 1988 text—in current use, they have been replaced by "Indigenous" / "First Nations, Métis, Inuit," "Secwépemc," "Nlaka'pamux," "St'at'imc," and "Tsilhqut'in." Still, "Indian" remains, in some cases: the "Indian Act" persists as Canada's apartheid law, and that word carries with it both history and a clear need for action. And, in Canadian law and history, "Indian residential schools" will forever be Indian, never Indigenous.

A FEW WORDS ABOUT THE TITLE
AND THE AUTHORS

When Randy, Brian, and I first began our discussion about a new edition of *Resistance and Renewal*, we were intending to keep the original title. But as our conversations deepened, I found myself seeking the wisdom of fluent Secwepemctsín speaker Garry Gottfriedson. We talked for hours, and I sent some thoughts to him in December after one of our FaceTime calls.

> I am thinking of what we talked about yesterday. "Revisited" is the word that came to my mind first, as we really are going back to the book and back to the stories that the people told me. But somehow this new book feels more than that. Circling back. And

then you said, "Circling back to *move forward*." And that really works for me ...

The building of relationships over time is always about circling back. And I continue to be amazed at how the people I have been thinking of over the years but not necessarily seeing are so welcoming, and we pick up where we left off. Sometimes with their kids that I knew as babies, even. So, for me, this work is a full circle. I started my academic career with the stories my First Nations friends and their relatives gave to me. And now I return to those stories and the people as I get ready to fade into the sunset. (Well, maybe not this moment, but you know ...) Even my work with you. From our grade 10 classroom to our beautiful conversation/collaboration yesterday.

Garry pondered for weeks, searching and researching for the word that would do justice to the return to these powerful stories and the people who told them. And one day, there it was: tsqelmucwílc, "we return to being human." We laughed with delight and danced for joy. Randy and Brian approved, and we added the subtitle: "Kamloops Indian Residential School" provides specific context, "resistance" maintains the original focus on the students' strength and creativity in the face of oppression, and "a reckoning" acknowledges both the return to the time and place of KIRS and the added commentary from survivors.

This brings me to the word "survivor," now an integral part of the authorship. As I pondered its use, Randy wrote,

I appreciate the word "survivor" because I survived the hellhole. Most of the people I started with in grade 1 are dead from violent deaths. To me, the word represents surviving the hellhole and surviving the impacts of what we were forced to live with, even if it is mostly in our memories. These memories affect our psyche, our mental well-being, our physical health, and our spiritual and emotional health.

Publisher and former Alberni Indian Residential School student Randy Fred at the *Resistance and Renewal* book launch, 1988.

Former KIRS student Anna Michel at the *Resistance and Renewal* book launch, 1988.

Each survivor had to find ways to suppress the overpowering sense of worthlessness forced upon them while at school. I never hear the word "survivor" without thinking of the late, great Haudenosaunee lawyer and scholar Patricia Monture-Angus. She wrote of being first a victim, then a survivor, next a warrior, and then, in her later writing, a teacher. The people who have shared their stories in this book and in the original version are just that—teachers for those who take the time to listen and learn. Years ago, Chippewa scholar Gerald Vizenor introduced a related word, "survivance," which he says moves beyond "a minimalist clinging at the edge of existence" and goes beyond mere survival (Vizenor 2008, 20). "Native survivance stories are renunciations of dominance, tragedy, and victimry" (Vizenor 1999, vii).

Survivors, survivance, teachers, and a return to being fully human—this book pays tribute to those who have survived Canada's efforts at cultural genocide and who, in the fullness of their humanity, continue to be willing to teach truth and to take action.

SOME HISTORY OF THIS BOOK

The research for the earlier text embedded within this book— *Resistance and Renewal: Surviving the Indian Residential School*— was conducted between December 1985 and June 1986. Residential schools have always been an issue for the people from the four nations who attended them (all "Indians" as defined by the Indian Act). But back then, few were talking openly about what the schools meant to them. The stories often remained hidden in memories because they were too painful to articulate or out of the belief that that was just the way things were. Those were the exact words of Gayle Gottfriedson, the daughter of original participant Mildred, in the summer of 2021: "I didn't talk about my time there. I always thought that was just the way things were."

Since 1986, many, many more stories have surfaced. Agnes Jack's *Behind Closed Doors* documents the personal healing journeys of former students of KIRS. Other books by Indigenous authors, from

Basil Johnston's *Indian School Days* in 1988 to Shirley Sterling's *My Name Is Seepeetza* to Bev Sellars's *They Called Me Number One*, augment and complicate our understandings of Canadian residential schools. And, of course, the Truth and Reconciliation Commission documented thousands of testimonies from across the country in their reports published in 2015. Many more books remain to be written, and many more stories remain to be told.

When I was working in the Kamloops area in preparation for the original book, I hoped it would be more than an academic exercise. I wanted the time and energy that those survivors/teachers offered me in their interviews to be useful to others. If I learned my lessons well, perhaps I could put these stories into some form that would allow others to share in their richness and insight. People who were ignorant of this aspect of Canada's history might come to see what it meant for those who had experienced it. That was my wish then. And so it remains.

Resistance and Renewal has had some success. In its three decades in print, it has been used in university courses from anthropology and education to history and law. Over the years, I have met and talked with First Nations people who have read it, and many acknowledge the similarity of their own experiences, whether they attended school in Fraser Lake, the Kootenays, Port Alberni, or any of the other schools across Canada. Some have asked for advice on documenting their specific experiences. Many others have now written their stories.

The book was criticized, particularly by clergymen, some historians, and sociologists who had been looking for something different, something perhaps less focused on the personal, representing perspectives other than those of former students, but had not found it in my book—though, as I noted above, I did occasionally nod in the direction of positivistic research. They found instead a retrospective ethnography that focused on the fact that all those interviewed shared the experiences of having attended the Kamloops Indian Residential School, having a significant prior relationship with the author, and being willing to talk about their experiences. During the interviews, I had recognized certain predominant perceptions and persistent attitudes, regardless of what time the students had attended. Even those who remembered the school as their only source of food and shelter at the time found their lives disrupted and affected in other ways by the long-term effects of separation from family, community, culture, and language.

Then Secwépemc chief Manny Jules at the *Resistance and Renewal* book launch, 1988.

Resistance and Renewal was also criticized by some Indigenous people who see my ongoing work as an unwanted intervention in Indigenous business. But for me, it has always been important to remember that the story of the schools is one in which non-Indigenous people played a central role. Some non-Indigenous people have said these stories are essential for all people who want to know the history of Canada. The Latin American Jewish feminist Judit Moschkovich says, "It is not the duty of the oppressed to educate the oppressor." People should find and read existing materials, she says, so that when the opportunity arises, they can engage in informed conversations with those whose voices have been too long excluded from mainstream histories and everyday understandings of what Canada is and how it came to be. I think of the strength and commitment of the people with whom I spoke, those who gave me pieces of their lives to put on paper for others to read. Together, we hoped to contribute to a more complete understanding—and ultimately, to more equitable treatment—of Indigenous peoples.

The structure of the book makes a clear distinction between what the people said to me and my interpretations. That is important for those who would search for other possibilities within the words. On the other hand, I find the interpretations I chose as appropriate and useful now as I did then.

Sexual abuse in residential schools became a major focus of court action and therapeutic work for survivors. It also became an endless source of sensationalism for the media. People did talk to me about abuse, usually after the tape recorder was turned off. Out of respect for those who did not want their words recorded, I included only some general statements about the abuse they mentioned. It is important to reiterate that sexual assault in all its horror was only one aspect of the abuse that the children in these schools endured. While it was devastating for so many, it remains but one facet of a fully abusive context in which Indigenous people's knowledge, languages, spiritual beliefs, and entire way of life were questioned and negated. Indigenous people were expected to emulate non-Indigenous people, though within limits; they were pushed off their lands, which were handed over to settlers and exploiters, and expected to serve as human resources for developing industrial Canada.

Throughout the onslaughts described in the stories that follow, Indigenous people resisted and found strength within that resistance. Aspects of their family teachings persisted—enough to build on, enough to feed the renewal process, which continues through governmental dithering, including constitutional restructuring, setbacks in land claims negotiation, and myriad other struggles. The gains of resistance are significant; there is no going back. Some of the determination that Indigenous peoples now exhibit had its roots in resistance to the invasive culture of the schools that was designed to annihilate Indigeneity; this resistance in turn was more deeply based in the long history and traditions growing out of respectful relation to the lands and waters. Down through the generations, resistance continues in the contributions made especially for this revised book.

In the 1970s, I saw the strength in the Secwépemc people in the Kamloops area as they continued the process of taking control of their education. I knew the stories of the residential school and wondered how their current active commitment to transforming education had arisen from such oppressive circumstances. Some of the answers lie in the powerful commentaries found in this book. It is the power to resist and to maintain a sense of culture, despite all odds, that brings Indigenous people to the reaffirmation of their knowledges and their ways of life, which are increasingly evident in Canada today.

Introducing the Original Text

F ew extensive studies of residential schools in British Columbia existed when the first edition of this book was published. Literature dealing with Indigenous education was based primarily on materials written by Euro-Canadians, with only minimal involvement from the people they wrote about. The few materials available that mentioned residential schools most often presented information from the perspectives of the government or of the missionaries whose policies directed and controlled them. The purpose of the book was primarily to present First Nations perspectives of the Kamloops

Kamloops Indian Residential School buildings. |
Kamloops Museum and Archives, 1987.013 002

Indian Residential School and to provide a limited introduction to the ways in which Indigenous education was evolving.

Thirteen interviews with former students of the school, First Nations people of the central Interior of British Columbia, form the nucleus of the original study. The fact that Interior people traditionally have oral cultures and that, for the most part, participants were previously known to the researcher made interviews in the form of conversations the most appropriate research approach. Drawing on the study participants' own words, the experiences of leaving home, arriving at school, surviving the daily routines of the school, resisting the oppressive structures imposed, and finally, returning home, are interpreted through the author's eyes and experiences. The analysis of the people's words came to focus on two concepts of paramount importance: cultural invasion and resistance.

Participants attended the school at various times. The author made a conscious effort to include male and female views, positive and negative views, and the views of students who attended for longer and shorter time spans. In addition, people from a number of different Secwépemc communities, and from communities beyond the Secwépemc Nation, agreed to speak with the author. Drafts of the manuscript were returned to the interviewees to allow for editing and to ensure their approval of the author's analysis and interpretation. Background information on the three groups involved with the school—students of the four First Nations, the missionaries, and the governments—was obtained from various archives and libraries.

The most outstanding feature the study revealed is the extent and complexity of the resistance movement that the students and their families developed against the invasive goals of the residential school. The struggles for power and control within the school may be seen as a microcosm of the ongoing struggles of Indigenous peoples with the Euro-Canadian presence in this country.

The need to develop positive relationships with one another, based in authentic dialogue and different from the hierarchical (and racist) ones that church, state, and academics too frequently have attempted to impose upon Indigenous people, is clear. Reconciliation may be a starting point for some to find ways to engage in real conversation with one another. Even at this time in 2022, implications for further research and writing are numerous—from specific aspects of culture, such as the historical role of arranged marriages and current strides in language maintenance and retention, to deeper considerations, such as the intergenerational impact of residential schools and contemporary Indigenous education. Ultimately, what emerges is a picture of strong individuals in a strong culture growing, adapting, and surviving.

CHAPTER 1

Setting the Scene

Three things stand out in my mind from my years at school: hunger; speaking English; and being called a heathen because of my grandfather.

—GEORGE MANUEL (MANUEL AND POSLUNS 1974, 63)

The Secwépemc, previously referred to as Shuswap, were traditionally a migratory hunting, fishing, and gathering people (Dawson 1891; Teit [1909] 1975). The people were migratory in that they travelled seasonally to traditional food-gathering places. Because of the severe winter climate of the surrounding Kamloops region, the other seasons were devoted to food gathering and preservation. In the summer and fall, people travelled to and camped at salmon fishing grounds to catch and dry fish. Throughout the growing seasons, they gathered berries and roots from designated places and dried them or used them in the preparation of food and the manufacture of utensils such as baskets. Hunting, a most important activity, was carried out through most of the year and often involved travel over great distances. Within Secwépemc society, all the complexities of culture existed: governance, spirituality, science, technology, acknowledgment and celebration of life passages, traditions, and oral history, which included a theory of origin. As with all cultures, language served as an expression of and for the transmission of an ever-evolving culture.

Into this relatively stable and thriving culture came the white European. Initially encounters were limited to exchanges with itinerant fur traders who had little effect on the lifestyle of the people who met them. Most often the Secwépemc were the ones who assisted the travellers with navigating and surviving the unknowns of their lands. Trade goods that enhanced or made easier the work of the First Nations people were taken up with relish. As European markets became more demanding and the West became more familiar, the North West Company began its push to establish trading posts to centralize efforts, increase profits, and reduce the travel of employees (Fisher 1977). In 1812, close to the site of a winter village of Secwépemc, Fort Thompson was founded at the confluence of two rivers known to the Europeans as the North and South Thompson.

About the same time, the Oblates of Mary Immaculate were intensifying their presence in British Columbia following a somewhat disappointing time in what is now Washington state. Lack of support from the American government dampened the enthusiasm of those in control, and BC became the target of a new missionary thrust toward Indian people (Cronin 1960, 46). Approximately sixty years after the founding of Fort Thompson, St. Louis Mission became a centre of operation.

During their involvement in the Pacific Northwest, the Oblates had become acquainted with and, on many occasions, immersed in the lives of First Nations peoples. Because of the limited number of priests and brothers working, one can assume that in order to minister more efficiently, the Oblates viewed the First Nations people's settlement into an agrarian lifestyle as a positive step. Indeed, in their moves to "Christianize and civilize" First Nations peoples, the Oblates viewed the acquisition of farming skills as progress—one in line with white European expectations. The migrant lifestyle of First Nations peoples, because it was different from European settler ambitions, was seen as inherently inferior.

The introduction of Catholicism to the Secwépemc was in some ways a relatively easy process, largely because of parallels between Secwépemc spirituality and aspects of the Catholic religion. While these were far from precise, spiritual beings similar to God, the Father, and Christ, his Son, were recognized by the Secwépemc.

> The Shuswap believed in two great spirits they called the Old-One and Coyote. The Old-One ... was all powerful.... The Old-One had as his chief assistant ... a spirit called Coyote. Although the description of Coyote varies somewhat from the Christian idea of Jesus ... there were enough similarities between the two figures to ensure familiarity for the Indians. Coyote was sent by the Old-One to travel over the world and put it to rights. (Whitehead 1981, 29–30)

Other similarities include the celebration of recurring annual festivals—Christmas/mid-winter, spring/Easter, and midsummer—and the recognition of individual guardian spirits. The differences, of course, far outweigh these similarities, but more than one person has commented that melding the two forms of spirituality is only a minor challenge.

Initially, the missionaries passed through the Secwépemc territory, preaching and converting. Shortly after BC's entry into Confederation in 1871 and the Oblates' establishment of the St. Louis Mission in 1878 (Morse 1949, 3) and a convent school for white girls that allowed Indian[5] girls to attend in 1880, the desirability of setting up an industrial school crystallized. As a continuation of the policy direction established by the Acts of 1868 and 1869, the federal government saw the schools as essential to educating the "Indian" to an agrarian lifestyle and ultimately to assimilate into the "superior" European society. The Oblates soon recognized the advantages of working with children in isolation from the influence of their parents and the importance of daily religious participation and instruction in moulding young minds. These two forces—church and government, supported by the Canadian people—have had the strongest cultural impact on the First Nations people in and around the Kamloops area.

THE GOVERNMENTS

The Province of Canada in 1847 published a report based on the ideas of Egerton Ryerson, which formed the basis for future directions in policy for Indian education and which, with Confederation, strongly influenced the development of schooling for Indians in British Columbia (Prentice and Houston 1975, 218). Clearly expressed is the perception of superiority of the European culture, the need "to raise [the Indians] to the level of the whites," and the ever-increasing pressure to take control of land out of Indian hands. At the same time, the contradictory need to isolate Indians from the evil influences of white society is acknowledged. The general recommendations of the report were that Indians remain under the control of the Crown rather than the provincial authority, that efforts to Christianize the

---

5 Throughout the original text, the word "Indian" is maintained and refers to those people defined as "Indian" under the Indian Act, a piece of Canadian legislation that remains in place to this day.

Indians and settle them in communities be continued, and finally that schools, preferably manual labour ones, be established under the guidance of missionaries (Prentice and Houston, 220). Cultural oppression was becoming written policy. Within the discussion of the recommendations is the following comment:

> Their education must consist not merely of the training of the mind, but of a weaning from the habits and feelings of their ancestors, and the acquirements of the language, arts and customs of civilized life. (Prentice and Houston, 220)

What clearer statement of an effort to destroy a culture could exist? The necessity of minimizing parental influence, another tool of cultural destruction, is further developed by Reverend Peter Jones, a First Nations convert to Christianity, in the same report:

> It is a notorious fact, that the parents in general exercise little or no control over their children, allowing them to do as they please. Being thus left to follow their own wills, they too frequently wander about the woods with their bows and arrows, or accompany their parents in their hunting excursions. (Prentice and Houston, 221)

The activities described were one of the main forms of traditional education for Indigenous people; children learned by observing and following their parents and by doing the same tasks expected of adults.

Following the establishment of the Indian Act of 1876, a consolidation of existing legislation, the government commissioned Nicholas F. Davin to report on industrial schools established for Native Americans in the United States. Out of his report came the strong recommendations that resulted in the establishment of many residential schools across Canada, including the one at Kamloops, British Columbia. In the introduction to the report, Davin made references to President Grant's policy on the "Indian question": "The industrial school is the principal feature of the policy known as 'aggressive civilization'" (Davin 1879, 1). Other comments show that some of Davin's attitudes were reinforced by politicians involved with schools for Native Americans. One point that frequently arose in discussions of Indian education was that working with adults or children in day schools was ineffective.

> The experience of the United States is the same as our own as far
> as the adult Indian is concerned. Little can be done with him....
> The child, again, who goes to a day school learns little, and what
> he learns is soon forgotten, while his tastes are fashioned at home,
> and his inherited aversion to toil is in no way combatted. (Davin, 2)

While positively endorsing the notion of residential schools for Indians in Canada, Davin's final comment is "if anything is to be done with the Indian, we must catch him very young" (12).

Several amendments to the Indian Act of 1876 occurred before the implementation of Davin's recommendations. One amendment regarding schools in 1880 is significant in that it typifies government's contradictory approach to input from bands. Even something as straightforward as the teacher's denomination is not left to chance.

Chiefs could henceforth frame laws in the following areas:

> 1. As to what denomination the teacher of the school established
> on the reserve shall belong to; provided always, that he shall be of
> the same denomination as the majority of the band; and provided
> that the Catholic or Protestant minority likewise have a separate

school with the approval of and under regulation's to be made by
the Governor in Council. (Miller et al. 1978, 78)

What appears at first glance to give some autonomy to the chief
actually contains such confining conditions that the choice is essen-
tially already made.

In 1887, Lawrence Vankoughnet, then deputy superintendent
general of Indian Affairs, again stressed the need for schools for Indian
children. He wrote to the Right Honourable John A. Macdonald:

> That the country owes to the poor Indian to give him all that will
> afford him an equal chance of success in life with his white brother,
> by whom he has been supplanted (to use no stronger expression)
> in his possessions, goes without saying, and the gift for which we
> pray on his behalf, with a view to the discharge of this just debt,
> is the education of his children in such a way as will put beyond
> question their success in after life. (Vankoughnet 1887, 1)

This report recommended the establishment of day schools.
By 1920, amendments to the Indian Act included compulsory school
attendance of Indian children and industrial or boarding schools for
Indians (Miller et al. 1978, 115). Following these amendments were
other minor ones relating to education. It is interesting to note that
in 1920, in the House of Commons' discussion of changes to the
Indian Act, Deputy Superintendent General Duncan Campbell
Scott stated clearly the idea that Indian cultures as such were to be
eliminated.

> Our object is to continue until there is not a single Indian in
> Canada that has not been absorbed into the body politic and

there is no Indian question, and no Indian department, that is the whole object of this Bill. (Miller et al., 114)

Not until 1946 was there a serious possibility for change in this attitude and in the express intent of Department of Indian Affairs policy. J. Allison Glen, minister of Mines and Resources, declared, "The Indian … should retain and develop many of his Native Characteristics, and … ultimately assume the full rights and responsibilities of democratic citizenship" (Miller et al., 130). Also in 1946, discussions began for complete revamping of the Indian Act. For the first time, and only after initial strong resistance by committee members, First Nations input was actually permitted. Andrew Paull, president of the North American Indian Brotherhood, appeared before the Special Joint Committee. He was highly critical of the committee's lack of First Nations representation. He condemned the existing Act as "an imposition, the carrying out of the most bureaucratic and autocratic system that was ever imposed upon any people in this world of ours" (Special Joint Committee 1947, 247). He spoke strongly for Indian self-government, finally commenting that what was needed was

> to lift up the morale of the Indians in Canada. That is your first duty. There is no use in passing legislation about this or that if you do not lift up the morale of the people. The only way you can lift up the morale of any people is to let the members look after themselves and look after their people. (Special Joint Committee, 427)

His words, delicately addressing the ongoing debilitating racism of Canadian society, fell upon deaf ears.

In 1947, anthropologist Diamond Jenness told the committee what it wanted to hear. His "Plan for Liquidating Canada's Indian Problems within 25 Years" (Special Joint Committee, 310–11) recommended the abolition of Indian reserves and the establishment of an integrated educational system as the basis for assimilation. The never-ceasing attempt by the now dominant majority society to make the Indian disappear continued unabashed through this revision of the Indian Act. "The new Indian Act did not differ in many respects from previous legislation" (Miller et al., 149). It did, however, serve as the beginning of the end for many residential schools, because it allowed for Indian attendance in the public school system.

MISSIONARIES

Secwépemc leader and author George Manuel writes, "All areas of our lives which were not occupied by the Indian agent were governed by the priest" (Manuel 1974, 63). Such was the case with the residential school. While the government espoused assimilation of the Indian through Christianization and civilization, it turned over the carrying out of the task to the religious orders—priests, nuns, and some lay teachers.

The Oblates of Mary Immaculate was founded in 1816 by Eugène de Mazenod in France. He sought to improve the quality of priests and of religious instruction while asking members of the order to emphasize self-spiritual regeneration, strict observation of the rules of the order and, secondarily, preaching to the poor. Original involvement with North America came in response to a request from the bishop of Montreal. From there, a small group of Oblates moved west, arriving in Oregon in 1847. Here, the philosophies that would guide much of the Oblate missionary work in British Columbia were put into action. In his "Instructions on Foreign Missions," de Mazenod wrote,

> Every means should therefore be taken to bring the nomad tribes to abandon their wandering life and to build houses, cultivate fields and practise the elementary crafts of civilized life. (Whitehead 1981, 118)

Second only to insisting that Indigenous people abandon their own spirituality and take up Christianity was the push for them to abandon their migratory lifestyle. From a practical point of view, it proved very difficult to minister to people who were frequently on the move.

Fort Kamloops, a North West Company trading post founded in 1812 and an important site of winter homes for the Secwépemc since time immemorial, was a logical site for the establishment of a mission. Father Demers, an Oblate, was the first missionary to visit the Kamloops area in 1842. In 1878, Father Grandidier was appointed rector and bursar of the permanent St. Louis Mission, with Father Chirouse directing. The original church and mission were located two and a half miles west of the present city centre. Father LeJacq then served as supervisor from 1880 to 1882 and was succeeded by Father Lejeune in 1883. In 1893, the Oblates took control of the recently established Kamloops Industrial School. Father A.M. Carion served as the principal of the school and, with some time away, remained in charge until 1916. While the priests frequently travelled to preach to the First Nations communities in the area, their policies served to control the direction of the school. In a report from Kamloops Indian Residential School, Father Carion states,

We keep constantly before the mind of the pupils the object which
the government has in view ... which is to civilize the Indians and
to make them good, useful and law-abiding members of society.
A continuous supervision is exercised over them, and no infrac-
tion of the rules of morality and good manners is left without due
correction. (Cronin 1960, 215)

The prime objective of the Oblates was to control the lives of the
First Nations people spiritually and in terms of lifestyle. Although
their impact on the people was very different from the whiskey trade
and the profit-seeking exploitation of some Europeans, it remained
exploitative in that the Oblates created a growing need for themselves in First Nations people's lives. Because the missionaries had
more extensive knowledge of Jesus Christ than the First Nations
people, once converted, the First Nations had to rely on this source
of religious instruction. Furthermore, only priests could say Mass
and offer the sacraments essential to the practising Catholic.

In British Columbia, the missionaries and governments worked
hand in hand to deal with the "Indian problem." The government
must have seen the religious order's efforts to control as most beneficial. Rather than sending soldiers and guns to control the owners
of the land, the governments had the missionaries, who influenced
First Nations people to limit their movements, take up an agrarian
lifestyle, and abandon their cultures.

The Oblates noticed that they were much more effective with
First Nations people who had not been involved with the corruptive
influences of some white traders. In 1861, Father Chirouse wrote,

I find it much more difficult to reclaim and teach those who are
brought much in contact with the evil-disposed and immoral

among the whites than is the case with those who are differently situated. (Cronin, 139)

This recognition led to an even stronger push for control of First Nations people's lives. It was seen as an advantage to separate them from the white settlements and, in the beginning, even from the English language. In a letter to Father Lejeune in 1892, L.N. St. Onge states,

> I agree with you that to teach English to the Indian is too much of a task. Besides they always learn it too soon for their own good. Unfortunately, when the Indians come to know English, they are more disposed to have relations with the whites, and you know what the result is of their intercourse. No, no, teach them no English. Let them learn it how they may, and as late as possible.

Although his words suggest that acquisition of English is inevitable, one can assume that he hopes to have Christianity ingrained before exposure to the evil influences of white settlers.

Despite its good intentions, this desire for control over First Nations people—partially through segregation and more directly through the destruction of their traditional lifestyle—reveals the invasive nature of the Oblates' work. References to "my Indians" are frequent, and this possessiveness, while showing attachment to the people, also belittles and relegates them to possessions. Brazilian scholar Paulo Freire, in his discussion of cultural invasion, refers to well-intentioned professionals who invade not as a deliberate ideology, but as an expression of their upbringing (1970, 154). He goes on to point out that cultural invasion "always involves a parochial view of reality, a static perception of the world and the imposition of this world view upon another" (159). Robin Fisher summarizes missionary efforts as follows:

> Because the missionaries did not separate Western Christianity and Western civilization, they approached Indian culture as a whole and demanded a total transformation of the Indian proselyte. Their aim was the complete destruction of the traditional integrated Indian way of life. The missionaries demanded even more far-reaching transformation than the settlers and they pushed it more aggressively than any other group of whites. (1977, 144–45)

Education was seen as a primary tool for effecting this transformation. In a vein similar to the government's notion of "getting them while they are young," the Oblates saw tremendous possibilities for control in the establishment of residential schools. Here the students could be isolated from the cultural influences of their parents, and a daily, systematic inculcation of Christian theory and practice would be possible. Attempts to control became close to absolute in that students were expected to attend from August to June, and visits from home were strictly limited. In a reversal of St. Onge's earlier recommendation, the use of English became mandatory. Through efforts to prohibit the use of First Nations languages, the very base of culture was attacked, and cultural genocide became policy.

Mounts Paul and Peter and South Thompson River, with school buildings in the distance, ca. 1895. | *Kamloops Museum and Archives, 5785 (accession #1973.045b)*

In Kamloops, the permanent residential school was built on land purchased by the government at the edge of what is now the land of Tk'emlúps te Secwépemc. It is across the river from the town, providing the separation deemed optimal. In addition, it was several miles from the Tk'emlúps village itself. The government had refused to purchase the buildings owned by the Oblates some miles away because it was felt they were asking too much money and the site was prone to flooding. In 1890, three two-storey wooden buildings were completed at the present site, providing separate dormitories for boys and girls, a living area for teachers, classrooms, and a play area.

After a faltering start under the guidance of lay teacher Michael Hagan, the school was taken over by the Oblates in 1893. The Sisters of St. Ann also played a major role in working with the girls. Sister Mary Joachim started at the school in 1890 and left shortly after, but she returned in 1894, when the Oblates had taken over, and remained until her death in 1907 (Secwepemc Cultural Education Society 1977, 8).

The original wooden buildings: Kamloops Industrial School, ca. 1914. | *Kamloops Museum and Archives, 1745*

In 1923, a new brick building was completed to replace the one damaged by fire. Throughout most of its operation until its closure as a residence in 1978, the Kamloops Indian Residential School was guided by the Oblates, assisted by the Sisters of St. Ann. In the usual male-female hierarchy within the church, the Oblate priests controlled policy and served as administrators, while the Sisters were expected to work obediently as teachers, child care workers, and supervisors along with the Oblate brothers, the labourers of the order.

Most students who attended the school fell within the governmental jurisdiction called the Kamloops Agency. This area included the southern Shuswap (Secwépemc) Bands of Bonaparte (St'uxwtéws), ChuChua (Simpcw), Skeetchestn, Kamloops (Tk'emlúps te Secwépemc), and the Sexqéltkemc te Secwépemc (Neskonlith, Adams Lake, Little Shuswap, Splatsin, and Shuswap), and several bands of the Thompson First Nation (now Nlaka'pamux) of the Nicola Valley (Scw'exmx). People from Scw'exmx could choose to send children to St. George's School in Lytton if they were Protestant or to St. Louis Mission in Kamloops if they were Catholic. In addition, some children from the Chilcotin (Tsilhqut'in) and coastal bands attended the school. Following the 1916 McKenna-McBride Commission hearings, day schools were built on several reserves located some distance from Kamloops. Rising birth rates and enforced attendance after 1920 provided students not only for these schools, but also for the residential school.

THE SECWÉPEMC

The Secwépemc whose children enrolled at that first residential school in 1893 had little experience with the formal European style of schooling offered by the Oblates. They saw childhood and schooling as an inseparable part of the ongoing process of life and living.

The methods used to teach skills for everyday living and to instill values and principles were participation and example. Within communities, skills were taught by every member, with Elders playing a very important role. Education for the child began at the time he or she was born. The child was prepared for their role in life whether it be food gatherer, hunter, fisherman, parent or knowledge-keeper. This meant that each child grew up knowing their place in the system.... Integral to the traditional education system was the participation of the family and community as educators. (Jack 1985, 9)

While warning of the dangers of generalizing, Mary Ashworth (1979) says of traditional education among the diverse tribal groups in British Columbia,

Education was the responsibility of all and it was a continuous process. Parents, grandparents and other relatives naturally played a major role, but other members of the tribe particularly the elders helped to shape the young people. (6)

In the early part of this century, James Teit, an ethnographer who learned Secwepemctsín (the language) and spent his life working with Indigenous peoples of the central Interior of British Columbia, wrote extensively of the Secwépemc people's traditional lifestyle. Children had few responsibilities or duties until they reached puberty. Although Teit does not comment in detail on Secwépemc childhood, he points out that children of the Nlaka'pamux, a closely related tribe to the south, had few restrictions. They had to rise early, wash frequently in cold water, and limit their play after sunset. Secwépemc children also participated in a complex ceremony twice a year called "whipping the children," in which they were encouraged to overcome fear and ultimately demonstrate courage (Teit [1900] 1975, 308–309). Otherwise, puberty was the time when they focused on training. Girls were assisted by a grandmother, mother, or aunt and spent a year in isolation practising all the work that women had to do. Boys, who isolated themselves for shorter periods of time, followed a similar pattern when their voices changed or when they dreamed of women, arrows, and canoes, but their training could last several years (Teit, 587–590). In addition to this specialized training, in the evenings Elders spent much time telling stories that emphasized ethical concepts and myths important to the people. Frequently, time was spent addressing the young people directly. "These were the times when the old people would address the young, and then they would admonish them to follow the rules of proper ethical conduct" (Teit, 617).

The startling differences between Secwépemc education and that of the residential school are numerous. Education for the Secwépemc was a responsibility shared by family and community. Only at puberty were children removed from the community for any length of time, and education was generally ongoing, not focused specifically on young people. The myths and stories told by the Elders were directed not only at children, but were also a part of the lifeblood of the community. The residential school, however, removed children from their community, placed them in large groups, and expected them to follow a tight schedule. The adults they had contact with had very definite ideas about the children's need for changes in language, beliefs, and lifestyle. The oppressive nature of residential religious schooling becomes clear.

Kamloops Industrial School girls, ca. 1918. | *Kamloops Museum and Archives, J.H. Clements fonds #2018.136.002 Photo Album, Photo #81*

CHAPTER 2

From Home to School

There was a lot more to our traditional education than just some Mickey Mouse courses in moccasin making.

—NISGA'A ELDER (MERKEL N.D., N.P.)

AT HOME

The Shuswap children who attended Kamloops Indian Residential School experienced many aspects of traditional family life and learning before they were taken to the school. As with all children, these initial experiences had a significant impact on their feelings about the residential school, both at the time they attended and in the long term. The former students' memories of their lives as children before they went to school reveal much about these varying effects.

The thing that I can remember about that little sod roof—it was like heaven to me, I guess, 'cause it was so full of love and happiness, freedom. We'd help my grandma pack her wood, and then she'd cook us something to eat. Then in the evening, she very seldom put a light in there because we didn't need a light.... At one end of that little sod roof ... they pegged some little sticks or posts across, just so high, and they put boards. And they filled it with that slough hay, full of that mint grass, and that bed used to smell so nice. She would put a tarp over it and then quilts, and that's where we all slept.

And my grandma would sit down, she had so much patience, I guess because she loved us so much.... She had a habit of always massaging our heads ... she'd rub our backs. And she would start telling us little legends.... Sometimes we would hear the same legend over and over, but I guess the lessons in those legends is what she was trying to get across to us.... At the end of the story, she would say "Tat a maa," which meant "See that man"—this is what would happen if you don't do it or you do it.

To me, when I look back, I can see me, especially in the spring when the little birds come back and you can hear them—makes you feel so good—and I could just see me running around, trying to catch a butterfly. And we never had bought shoes, we always had moccasins all the time. And I guess those were the nicest, most beautiful times of my whole life ... that freedom, my life so full of love. (Sophie)

Within these words of remembrance are several life values of great importance to First Nations people: the extended family exemplified by the grandmother and her teaching through story; familial patience and love; the associations with natural mint grass, butterflies, and freedom; and the contributions of even the littlest child to the work of the household. Life before residential school was seen as an idyllic, carefree time by most of the people interviewed. Not all play, it was also a time of learning small and then larger tasks, such as cooking, splitting and packing wood, felling trees, and mowing hay. Traditionally, the children took on more and more work as they grew and were able to manage more, learning by watching and doing.

First of all, I sensed there was an expectation for me to do those [things], and because of that I started watching.... I learned how to chop wood after observing my father, my grandfather, and my mother chopping wood and how safety conscious they were in taking care of the axe and making sure that no harm will be done. I would try on little pieces of wood, maybe the kindling, and if they did notice me holding the axe the wrong way, then they would point out the right way to do it.

We followed Dad while he worked on the farm mowing hay.... [In] playing, we also knew why he stopped the machine—it was plugged up—and what he did to clear it. He didn't use his hands; he used a stick to clear away in case the horses moved.... We did that as a game not so much as direct learning.... Around about seven or eight [years old], he said to us, "I want you to take a round" ... and maybe that will be all for a year.

As a logging contractor, he went up the hill, and he'd invite us as youngsters ... to be with him. We need not do anything ... but I imagine his purpose was for us to watch him do things—how to cut a log so it will fall a certain way. (Joe)

For some people, particularly those who had large families and did not go to school until the age of nine or ten, the work was more arduous.

Coming from a large family, we all had chores to do as soon as we were able to pick up anything, and then there was always a baby. Being the oldest ... there I was at the age of seven, six ... already babysitting.... I even helped doing the diapers and feeding the baby.... And then we worked out in the garden, we packed wood, we done all these chores. (Josephine)

One man who started at residential school in 1958 at the age of ten reported that his mother kept him out of school so that he could help with all his little brothers. He was also expected to help with all the household chores, including washing clothes and doing dishes. Yet he remembered this time as one of freedom. While his memories may be influenced by the contrast between his early life and the oppressive system he was later subjected to, this sense of things being positive remains strong in his mind.

For some, life before school was not all security. In the 1950s, a generation of people who had attended the residential school and thus had little opportunity to learn parenting skills came to parenthood; along with the influence of alcohol, this created some unhealthy situations for children. The intergenerational effects of residential school began to take hold.

> My mom used to leave us, eh, and this one time she left us with this sitter. At the time, I used to trust everybody, and this time she left me with her uncle to babysit us.... My mom and dad wanted to go to the dance so they left, and this uncle of hers, he ... sexually abused me. I got to a point where I forgot about it and, well, I guess I hated the thoughts so much, I just forgot. I remembered after, and I didn't know whether I should tell my parents. I was really ashamed. (Anonymous)

This person felt that she must somehow be responsible for the abuse perpetrated by the adult charged with caring for her—this she now understands as the classic reaction of an abused child. Notably, incidents such as this one were rarely mentioned by people when they recalled their lives before school; rather, they emphasized a combination of having freedom to play and chores to do.

Grandmothers, as already mentioned, were major figures in educating the children. Traditionally, grandparents were teachers of the community as a whole as well as children in particular. To this day, knowledgeable Elders are respected as teachers.

> I felt good when I was with my grandmother. I felt like I was with nature, and I felt like I was with something that was rightfully mine.
>
> She taught me about nature, about myself, about my Indianness. She taught me all these things, and I think that gave me a lot of courage to be where I am today....
>
> The grandmother's teachings were very patient, you know.... I was taught how to make moccasins at an early age of eight, and I knew in later years my first pair of moccasins wasn't the best. But my grandmother praised me and told me, she says, "You just continue.... You are going to do better at it each time." Her beliefs of teachings was you try to do it on your own, try to think for yourself. Thinking back now, she was trying to tell me something ... and I kept on trying ... because I had so much love for my grandmother and great-grandmother.... I wanted to do more for them. (Mildred)

Along with the lessons and encouragement came other attributes of grandmothers.

> In the winter months, we loved staying with our grandmother because grandmothers have a habit of collecting a lot of goodies. I remember my grandmother used to have a box in the corner. We were not allowed to touch it. We were obedient; we never touched it because we knew we were going to get it anyway. And we were never hungry with my grandmother. If we were exceptionally

good ... she would reward us with the thing that I loved—that fruit leather. She used to pick wild raspberries, huckleberries, oh, any soft fruits. She'd take it and mash it and—by this time, she had tin plates—pour it in tin plates and set it out in the hot sun. It would form a crust on top and then she would flip it over, and it would form a crust on the other side, no sugar added to it. The inside would form into like a jelly and then she'd put them away.... What she used to do was break a piece off for us, and boy, we used to just love it. (Sophie)

Always there were lessons to be learned. Some came embedded in story, some as encouragement to attempt a task, and some as cultural subtleties developed through centuries of interaction with other Shuswap people.

My granny was forever, every time she went visiting her relatives or family, she always came back with bundles of goodies. And when her friends would come to visit her, she'd give them stuff.... That was one of the traditions, that when you went to visit your friend or your relative, you never left empty-handed. It was the idea of the nice feeling about giving.... The person you give it to respected you, even if she might have loads and loads of dried saskatoons or huckleberries or whatever, but it was the idea. It wasn't in big, large packages; it was in just little packages. It was the idea that you're going with a little gift; you're taking some-thing from that person.... Anyway, that was the type of thing that I learned when I was young. (Sophie)

These traditions were ingrained before the children went to school and were part of what contributed to the survival of the

Secwépemc people in spite of the onslaught of residential school training. Joe, now a teacher, recalled important pedagogy he learned from his grandmother.

> I had a grandmother who lived with us while our mother and father were away.... She was crippled ... so she would, from her bedside, tell us, "Fill the water three-quarters full. Turn the potatoes now to this level. Make fire." She provided that knowledge, and we just carried out the directions. But at the same time, when it was cooked and well done, we'd say, "Oh, I cooked," and that indirect way of learning was good because we were not doing it as a task, but we were doing it to help grandmother as if we were in some kind of partnership.... Next week, she would go out. She loved to go out for little walks and she would say, "Do you think you can handle cooking up to the end?" And I'd say, "Yes, I can." Oh, if we made the odd mistake, she'd come and fix it up. It gave us the security to go in there and do the best possible job we can. Generally, we were 70 to 80 percent correct, and she would recognize the 80 percent and not really focus on the 20 percent too much. That was her task; the 20 percent was hers to go in there and fix it up.... My younger brother would at times bake, and his proficiency level was 50 percent, but he felt good because Grandmother focused on the 50 percent. She'd say, "You did good up to this point. The rest is my job. I'll fix it up."

The emphasis on children observing tasks that would become part of their life work was another important method used by the Secwépemc. Young children went along and played, but at the same time began the duty of learning, first by observing and later by doing.

I went everywhere with [my grandmother]. And so by going everywhere with her, I was learning.... I think that was really where my education started.... I picked berries with her. I don't remember doing it yet I went with her, but she picked the berries and I goofed around, you know....

I may have watched her more than once do that in-the-ground cooking, that steam cooking, but I remember that one time that I watched her, I don't even think that I watched 100 percent. I remember looking for the rocks and her piling up all the things she was going to need, but I think when she was actually cooking the food, I must have been playing somewhere, but I remember eating it. (Charlotte)

Charlotte's grandmother died when she was seven, and she was subsequently sent to residential school. Clearly, these were the introductory lessons which could have been built upon as the child grew. In an extremely gentle way, the child was made aware of places to pick berries and ways to prepare and cook food. Sophie remembered an incident on a root-digging trip with her grandmother.

We used to go with her digging roots.... She had this mare that had this little colt, and she'd take the mare and she'd put all our bedding on the back of the mare and all of her baskets and all our food that we're going to take and maybe camp overnight. So we'd go with her. And ever since that colt was born, we used to handle it. It was so tame; as it grew bigger, we used to grab it. My grandma would be walking along with her cane, leading the horse, and we'd be running behind. And we would catch the little colt and we'd hang on to it, all three of us, and the colt was trying to get away. We'd wait until she got quite a ways, and one of us would get on and hang on for dear life. That little colt would run to beat heck, till soon it would catch up to its mother, and she would stop with a jolt, and over we'd go.

Both the root-digging expedition and the initial steps in riding and training horses were skills that equipped the children for adult life. Archie, reminiscing in his forties about his life before residential school, recounted that there were always plenty of horses to ride. This point he remembers above all others. Again, that which was expected to be important in adult life was introduced at an early age. For this man, horses have turned out to be his main occupation in life. Horses and horsemanship continue to be valued by and valuable to many Secwépemc people today.

Bedtime, always an important time for little children and of seldom discussed cultural significance, was a happy time—a communal time. The hay and mint grass mattress in one grandmother's cabin has already been described. Julie, in her late thirties, had this to say about bedtime:

> At home we only had two bedrooms. So the boys all slept in one bed, and the girls all slept in another bed. And Mum and Dad and whatever the baby was slept in Mum and Dad's room. So we were never, ever separate from one another. We done everything together, slept together, everything.

For some, the Catholic religion had already begun to play a major role in their lives. Partly because of apparent resonances with traditional Secwépemc spirituality and partly because of effective missionary work on the part of the Oblates, Catholicism quickly gained a foothold in much of the central region of the province.

> I knew all about the church.... My mum and dad were religious people; they were God-fearing people.... Before I went to school, I was already taught there was a God. My mum would point out a lot of things [and say], "You know, there is definitely a God." (Josephine)

Another student, Joe, recalled,

> The old priest referred to the ground right under us as his textbook, as his catechism.... He would just sit us down, sometimes we'd kneel on the floor or sometimes on his knee. He would say, "See the water, see the birds, see the sky, see the mountains. View each one because they were made by a greater being than us." ... And then he went into hurting and not hurting one another.... Of course, these too were taught by our chiefs.... One of the stock talks they would give would be to give thanks to the Creator for giving us the water, the trees, all the plants and animals, and all the resources of the earth—that they couldn't be made by man, that they had to be made by higher beings than us.

For the young children, these priests seem to have de-emphasized the concepts of guilt, confession, and forgiveness, which play prominently in Catholicism. Some interviewees spoke positively of the formal religion they experienced before residential school. However, most did not focus on religion, and no one spoke negatively of their experience with it before school.

Discipline by Secwépemc parents and grandparents was mentioned by most of the people with whom I spoke. Generally there was a minimum of physical punishment, but when needed, reprimands were seen as fair and effective.

> If you had chores to do ... you had better get them done. My mum
> very seldom gave us the strap. We just went back and done them
> and you just stayed there until you had finished them. (Josephine)

Even grandparents who were a little frightening did not resort to
physical abuse.

> My grandfather used to get mad at my mum and dad all the time
> because our parents left us with them so much. They got mad
> at us too, you know; they got tired of us.... I was really afraid of
> my grandpa then 'cause he used to holler lots.... No, they never
> spanked any of us. My grandma was really nice, though. (Beverly)

Charlotte, raised by her grandmother, recalled that her grandmother punished her severely on only one occasion. She had gone
to the washroom without her grandmother's permission during a
community dance and was watching, fascinated, as an older girl put
on lipstick, "When all of a sudden, *whack*, *whack*! And there was my
grandmother just tugging me out the door."

Anna reported that after she'd destroyed a number of plants in
a greenhouse, her mother demanded a reason, and she responded
that she had done it because she wanted to. Because she was honest,
she "never got a lickin' or anything. I didn't do it because I hated him
or hated her or anything. I [just] wanted to." In another incident,
Anna described what may be seen as the adult consequences of her
behaviour.

> Another time the same guy, he was teasing me, and I was across
> the heater and there was a poker there for the heater. He was
> teasing me, and I was mad.... I said, "I'll hit you with this." I took
> the poker, and he said, "Go ahead. Go ahead." And I did. I went

like this [gesturing]. *Boink.* He didn't think I would, and I did. He looks at my mum, and my mum never said anything. Finally, he said, "Aren't you going to do something about it?" My mum said, "What can I do? She told you she was going to hit you—you said to go ahead."

Interesting to note is that the person engaged in the altercation with the child was non-Indigenous. Clearly, he had not understood that children in Secwépemc culture were viewed as young adults in many ways, and that under these circumstances, he had made a serious error in judgment.

These stories highlight the important memories of home life before school for people who were destined for the Kamloops Indian Residential School (KIRS). Some of the carefree nature of life before school may be attributed to the fact that, without exception, the children had been no more than ten years of age and, therefore, still had limited responsibility. However, the tenor of a life closely connected with the natural world, the importance of the grandmother's presence and teachings—which in many cases continued to influence the children into adulthood—and the assumption that children are full-fledged contributing members of the household stand out as extremely important in the lives of these Secwépemc children.

Of particular significance is the resultant clash of these cultural notions with the systematized, European-influenced life of residential school. The rigid time schedules, the dearth of family contact even among siblings, and the constant supervision and direction accompanied by severe punishments for deviation were aspects of a way of life foreign to Secwépemc children.

Students and staff of KIRS, 1933. | *Kamloops Museum and Archives, 8014*

THE TRANSITION

Into the idyllic summer life of camping and berry and root gathering came the school truck. Out stepped a huge European man in black clothing with a list in his hand. The separation began.

> The school truck used to come with a little fence around the back, you know. Used to come, I think for Chase, it was August 30th, or was it the 31st? Anyway, they had me ready. My mum brought me, and everybody grouped around the truck. And I think it was Anthony Liah would have a list of names, and you went on up these little stairs as your name was called. (Anna)

Most people now refer to this school truck as the "cattle truck." For many children, it was their initial introduction to a way of life in which their family and cultural identity was obscured, their language became useless and even despised, and their personal identification was a number written in purple ink on their wrists and on the small cupboard in which their few belongings were stored. Not all stops were as orderly as the one described above. For some students, resistance to the imposed culture began with that initial contact. Julie described this horrific scene:

> I can remember Dad left really early that morning 'cause he never, ever wanted to see us go off to school. And when he left that morning at five, I tried sneaking out with him. He was really crying, my dad was. And he told me, "No, you stay. You got to go to school." And I just [said], "No, I want to stay with you. I want to stay with you." And I was crying just as hard as he was. Finally, I just wrapped my arms and legs right around him, and every time he went to take a step, he had to pack me with him 'cause I was hanging on to him so hard. He walked back in the house and pulled me off of him and sat me on the couch, and he finally yelled at me, "You sit right there and don't you move until them people come!" But he was crying. He walked out and he got on his horse and went and left. That was really hard to take, you know....
>
> When that truck did come, boy, I tell you. We had a back door and a front door, and we beelined it. I didn't know exactly where they were going, but when everybody started running, I started to run too and realized that the truck was there. And they literally chased us down....

And the kids that are on the truck, they're all bawling because they're seeing us, you know, screaming and yelling.... Of course, they're all crying because we're crying, and Mum's crying, and I can remember [saying], "What'd I ever do to you? Why are you mad at me? Why are you sending me away?" ... She was really heartbroken.

The confusion and distress on the part of both parents and children were clear. The painful process of cultural invasion, a systematic step that involved removing the children from the influence of their parents, had begun.

The school truck. "Of course, they're all crying because we're crying, and Mum's crying ..." | *Les Williams*

Although the "cattle truck" was the most frequently remembered travelling conveyance, some children came to school by other means. Minnie, who attended KIRS in 1907, when it was known as the Kamloops Industrial School, recalled,

> When our people bring us back to school, they go on the wagon a few days ahead. And they camp close to the river, on this side of the bridge. Lots of 'em do that. They got no car, just go on a wagon or a buggy. Take lots of lunch. When it's time to go back to school, they bring you to the school, the Indian school.

Certainly, this trip to school provided a temporary stay to the impending assault on the child's way of life by the agents of the government and church. Mildred remembered going to school by car.

> Out of the blue there comes this car, drove up to my mother and father's place. And my mother was dressing up my sister and I ... and my mother told us that we were going to be riding in that car ... and that we were going to go to school. We didn't know what a school was. I thought maybe we'd go there and come right back. And that was the most terrifying part of my whole life. It seemed like that car chugged along forever.... It took us seemed like a whole day and it seemed like we were gone to the other end of the world, and we'd never find our way home.

Mildred's story of fear is even more poignant when one knows that, following an incident much discussed in hushed tones by the adults of the community, she had been warned to run if she ever saw a white man. Suddenly, she found herself in a car with a strange European man, going where, she did not know. She heard years later that the incident had involved the rape of a young Secwépemc woman by three European men. The woman's baby, who had been strapped to her back, was smothered during the attack.

For some other children, going to school was a time of pleased anticipation. New school clothes brought great excitement to Beverly's introduction to school in the 1950s.

> What used to happen is our parents used to buy new clothes and then we were sent to school.... I think we went over on the bus, and I was kind of looking forward to this 'cause we're going on this trip with our brand new clothes. My sisters never even told me what it was like there.... They never talked about the school. And I wondered what it was going to be like. It was almost like a celebration coming up.... That was the greatest thing, to have new clothes.

The children who went to school willingly were older—nine or ten—and they usually had some understanding that, although their parents would miss them dreadfully, learning to read and write was of prime importance.

> My mum explained to me, when we discussed it ... she said, "I'm sending you to learn to read and write and to learn your catechism, to learn about God." ... So I knew why I was coming to school.
>
> My cousin Eliza was appointed to bring me.... I was apprehensive. I was wondering how it was going to be. I knew I was leaving my mum ... but we had discussed it so many times before, and it was happening, you know, it was real. But I guess with Eliza, on the bus, she just had such a hard time to keep from crying. (Anna)

This story holds two points of significance. The first is the fact that the child's mother had never attended residential school (or any other school), but her cousin Eliza had. Understanding what lay ahead for the child, Eliza felt considerable trepidation. The mother, on the other hand, recognized that some good could come of learning to read and write, which she saw as the goals of the school. Secondly, the older children whose parents explained the purpose of the school to them felt more comfortable with their journey there. In traditional education, these complex explanations were unnecessary, because teaching and learning were part of the natural flow of life. With the cultural onslaught of the residential school, though, parents were required to make a major adjustment to their way of dealing with their children in order to smooth the transition into a foreign culture. Only some recognized and responded to this need.

Upon their arrival at the school, undermining the children's culture began in earnest. Some of the clashes were deliberate, a part of the Oblates' plan and the government's mandate to "civilize and Christianize" Indigenous people. Others may have been well intentioned but demonstrated the lack of cultural awareness or sensitivity in the people in charge of the children. More than any other time at the school, memories of the first day lived vividly in the minds of every person interviewed.

> Coming to this huge, huge building, it staggered us. With eight of us in a home and sometimes ten, we lived in a one-room house.... It seemed, as we came into the building, we were just swallowed up by some strange being. Everything was strange, even the running water was strange. The bathroom was strange. The echo of the hallway was a noise I hadn't heard before, and the banging of doors from far away was strange. We came into a totally strange world. (Joe)

Another student, Mildred, remembered this scene:

All of a sudden, here we come in front of this building. And after being told to be afraid of white people, you can imagine the feeling we had. We were herded into the front and down the hall, where the dining room is. We were all standing there, my sister and I hanging on to each other. We were already so scared, and we were lonely for the protection of our parents. We didn't know what we were going to be getting into. [We wondered], "Why did my mother and father send us away?" And then, all of a sudden, we seen somebody coming down the hallway all in black and just this white face, and that's when I started just shaking and we all started crying and backing up.... We were doing that of sheer fright. This sister is coming towards us, and what has been going in her mind is, "Here's these little wild animals." You know when you go to touch a little wild animal, it cringes, and we say right away, "Oh, it's a wild animal. We've got to tame it." I could just imagine what was going on in her mind: "These little wild Indians, I've got to tame them." ... And here's me, I'm saying, "I'm so scared. What is she going to do to me?" And after hearing about them killing our own people, are they here to butcher us, or what are they going to do to us?

"Coming to this huge, huge building, it staggered us." |
Kamloops Museum and Archives, 1873

The school personnel's perception of Indian children as wild and animal-like is supported by comments made by the Oblates regarding their efforts to instill European values into the minds of Indigenous people. The first close-up view of the nuns brought fear to many children.

> I just couldn't get over these nuns wearing long black.... I was kind of scared of them; they looked so white. They had this little part of their face showing, everything else was covered ... their long beads rattled. When they walked, their little heels clicked

on the cement floor. Wherever they went, you could hear them walking because they had that heel and the little jangle. (Beverly)

Strange sights and strange sounds filled the children's first days of school.

Although many children came to the school in tears, the more defiant ones were dragged kicking and screaming from the truck.... The first day I went to that school, they had to literally carry me off the truck, and that nun, I have her outfit in shambles. I was calling her a witch and just kicking and screaming at her. I mean, I wasn't the only one; there was a lot of other kids that were doing that, and finally the head nun ... she had the strap and she went, *whack, whack* on the table.... "Okay, you kids," she said, "That's enough out of you or you're going to get this." (Julie)

For children who had rarely if ever experienced physical punishment, the threat of the strap must have been especially fearsome.

Once inside the school, students were often subjected to head checks before the mandatory haircuts.

We had to get in this line, and we had to get our heads checked for lice.... Some of the kids had to get their heads cleaned. And soon as they finished checking our heads, they cut our hair. They cut our hair in front like bangs above the eyebrows, side to side on your face here, by the temples ... and just right at the top part of your ear, it was cut straight around, and on the back where your neck is, it was cut so straight that the back parts here were shaved.... I think we practically all looked the same 'cause we all had the same haircut, the same-coloured clothes, and all had the same everything. (Beverly)

Along with the initial shock and fear of leaving their parents and entering into a strange world, the haircut added salt to their wounds. Traditionally, long and often braided hair played (and plays) an important role in recognized events, including puberty rites. Beverly's account makes explicit the feeling of loss of personal and cultural identity at a very sensitive time, as the children realized that they now "all looked the same." As for the school personnel, adherence to European norms of "civilization" required short hair for girls and shorter hair for boys—another aspect of cultural invasion.

Students and staff of KIRS, n.d. Notice the shaved heads and uniform haircuts. | *Kamloops Museum and Archives, 8016*

One might expect that information from family members and friends already attending the school might ease the transition for children. But, as has already been mentioned, it was common for siblings and friends not to discuss their school experiences at home. Presumably the pain of school was a topic to be avoided during time away from it. The incongruity between life at home and life at school did not encourage casual discussion. Built into the school's rigid structure were segregations that severely limited access to other family members. It remains unclear whether such separation of siblings and sexes was intentional—another means of assault on the strong family ties that might permit the maintenance of cultural commitments, including language—or merely a matter of convenience for the staff.

The children were divided into three gender-based age groups: juniors, for grades 1 to 3; intermediates, for grades 4 to 6; and seniors, for grades 7 and 8. Little social interaction was permitted between and among the groups. One student recalled her sister's first day at the school.

> I remember her really, really getting scared. You know, she was excited at the beginning, at home, feeling safe, having safe surroundings, and then from there she was taken with us on the bus all the way down here.... Her and I had to go in separate parts of the building, so I remember her clinging onto my arms when we were going up the stairs ... and she kept telling me in our language she didn't want to go.... She didn't know English very much, and the sisters yanked her away because I had to go to my room....
>
> I remember feeling very sorry for her and feeling like I couldn't help her very much, feeling helpless. I felt like I was put in a position to look out for her, but that didn't take form because she couldn't spend a week with me to adjust to the whole thing—me

telling her exactly what the routine was. But they didn't think of that; they didn't think of Indian kids' interests, I don't think.

Other people recollected that even though their sisters were in a room beside them, they could not visit one another. This separation of family members led to feelings of powerlessness, as expressed by the older sister above. For the Oblates' purposes and in light of traditional European schooling, this sense of powerlessness was appropriate to children whom they viewed as mere objects to be subjected to the treatment deemed fitting for them by their elders and betters. Of course, this approach is a direct contrast to the traditional Secwépemc view, which did not separate children from adults; rather, they were seen as fully participating members of a household, taking on tasks as appropriate to their abilities. That this change encountered at school created feelings of incompetence is clearly expressed in the following account:

> Before I left [home], I was full of confidence. I could do every-
> thing that was needed to be done at home.... But when I arrived
> here, all that left me. I felt so helpless. The Shuswap language was
> no use to me ... the supervisors couldn't understand. (Joe)

For Anna, as an older child coming to school, one of her first experiences there triggered an undermining sense of helplessness. Her initial hours at the school had been relatively comfortable: "I have no emotions yet, and you know, it's all new, and I have to keep my eyes open and learn." However, this healthy interest came to a rude end after the first supper.

> After supper, everybody had jobs.... And I'm standing there, you
> know, [thinking], "Where's everybody going? What's happening?"

And this sister called me and said, "You're new—you go to the recreation room." And I have no idea what the recreation room is, and I'm standing there.... Now, there is the first emotion I had. "What is she saying?" And she calls, "Clara, come here." So I looked back and here this little girl comes bouncing towards Sister. "Clara, you take Anna down to the recreation room and then you come back and do your work." And this little girl takes my hand—smaller than me, she's so bouncy and happy looking— she takes me, and I'm dying of shame that this little girl knows what this big word is and she knows where she is going to. Holy man, I mean what's the matter with me? Oh, I'm so ashamed. She takes me to the recreation room and says, "This is the recreation room," and she smiles at me and she leaves. And I go in there. I guess there are some more of us big dummies.

Although intended to be helpful, the sister's action violated a social rule. Not to know something and to be helped by someone obviously smaller and younger in front of other people was a public humiliation for Anna. To this day, many Secwépemc people see being shamed in public as an insult, a punishment. To Anna on that day so long ago, the interaction was devastating.

Not only were older and younger siblings separated, but in the spirit of old Catholicism, males and females were isolated from one another. Sexuality has often been viewed by conservative factions within the Catholic Church as an area which, unless strictly controlled, inevitably leads to sin. Initially, it resulted in the separation of brothers and sisters. More than one student reported seeing her brother only once or not at all during their years of attendance at the school.

Boys at Kamloops Industrial School, n.d. | *Kamloops Museum and Archives, Fernie Family fonds, #2007.004/005 (01)–(19), Mary Fernie Photograph Album v.3, file 11, Photo #1*

Most of the people interviewed commented that the introduction to life on the boys' side of the school was very rough. It is notable that few males wanted to speak about their experiences at the school, and those who did often preferred not to be identified or spoke off the record.

> The first night. I had three scraps on account of my brothers. You always got tested out. I showed them ... I was more outgoing, ready for anything on account of my [public] schooling over there. (Sam)

The boys' resistance to the system being imposed upon them took on a different form from the girls', which tended to be more subtle, though just as effective. In fighting the rules and regulations of the school, the boys developed a counterculture of clique-like groupings sometimes based loosely on community origins. Some boys who arrived later in September than the others ("I suppose they looked at their list, saw there was still room at the school, and they went back and got us"), found their introduction very trying.

> Do you know when we see pictures of muskox in a circle being attacked by wolves.... It seemed we were that.... We were in the center—four of us. Youngsters of all ages touching us and watching our reactions as we tried to grab or scratch or hit. As our backs were turned, somebody would grab us from the back. And we just wished we could return home to a more safe and secure place. (Joe)

Examination of the groupings that developed among the boys in their daily life at the school suggests that this initiation was part of the process of screening newcomers to determine their toughness. According to several interviewees, this type of behaviour was not typical of children's interactions at home, but came to the surface in the oppressive atmosphere of the school. One girl's brother had been to the school before her and had apparently tried to prepare his siblings for the type of treatment that they could be subjected to on arrival at school.

> My oldest brother, he wanted to prepare us for our life. Like he was teaching us how to fight, and he taught us that we shouldn't cry if something happened to us.... He wanted us to be tough. (Beverly)

Language, that aspect of culture so central to its expression and transmission, was a major issue within the school. With obvious understanding of the importance of eliminating this tool of culture, the Oblates began their attack on Indigenous languages during the children's first days at school and continued to escalate the conflict with those who did not cooperate in abandoning their language. For the children who spoke only Secwepemctsín upon their arrival at school, their first days were ones of gibberish, because older children were not permitted to speak the language, and few supervisors ever spoke Secwepemctsín. No transition time in which they might reach some understanding of the new language was allowed. One interviewee who entered the school at nine remembered,

> And knowing very little English, I had some difficulty with that. I got into trouble because of not knowing English and not speaking out or saying the wrong word, even being confused about yes and no.... One of the supervisors wrote our names and our numbers; we each had a school number on our wrist. So rather than answering in English, "What is your number? What is your name?" ... we would just show our wrist.... That was our identification; they wrote it in that purple pencil. (Joe)

For some, the first day of school was so full of new and often frightening experiences that the lack of language was not a major focus in our conversations. One person who did speak English when they arrived reported, "I don't think I did very much talking the first few days 'cause, you know, you had to get used to everything around here."

The final shock of the first day came at bedtime. Instead of communal beds, as they were accustomed to at home, the children were directed to dormitories containing rows and rows of individual beds, each with white sheets and a single blanket. For a few, this time was pleasant: "What I remember the most was getting into a bed of my own, and it had clean sheets. The place smelled great" (Mildred). Sam described his first night very differently: he recalled standing at the window, holding his two brothers' hands as they cried and gazed longingly toward their nearby home on the reserve. "I kept looking over there—freedom, what I used to do" (Sam). For another person, the sheets and pillow offered little solace.

> When they tried to put me to bed without my sister in this one bed with my own pillow, my own sheet, I didn't even think that was very nice. I couldn't believe that I didn't have nobody to sleep with. That I was going to have a bed all to myself sort of scared me, and I howled all night. (Julie)

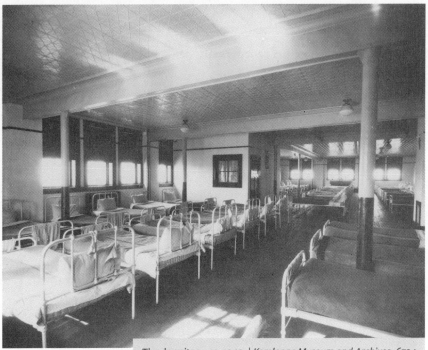

The dormitory, ca. 1940. | *Kamloops Museum and Archives, 6724*

Again, no recognition was given to the Secwépemc ways, and no allowance was made for a gradual introduction of European conventions. In a systematic and rigid fashion, the Oblates demonstrated that the Secwépemc cultural patterns were not acceptable in the school. In all aspects of life, from language to sleeping habits, European behaviours were to supplant those which had been followed by generations of Secwépemc. From these first days onward, no concessions were made; family ties were interrupted, language was forbidden, and prior life experience and knowledge were discounted.

As this oppressive system began to operate, glimmerings of a developing counterculture were also in evidence. In subtle and not so subtle ways, the children began the delicate balancing act of adapting to a new order while retaining the indelible aspects of their original culture and their sense of self. This resistance to the system, which resulted in the production of subcultures within the school, began in the very first days. The following example typifies the underground culture in operation as the student quoted above addresses the problem she encountered.

> I had to sneak to my sister's bed. She was in the same dorm as I was. I don't know who the girls were who were sleeping beside us, but they were going to squeal on us, and she up and told them she'd beat the living shit right out of them if they so much as said a word. She was classified as one of the tough girls, so they listened to her. (Julie)

While cultural invasion had begun in earnest, the forces of opposition were also forming ranks. It is this strength of resistance that has ensured the survival of the Secwépemc people as a nation today, despite the efforts of both governments and missionaries to undermine their cultural roots and make them an indistinguishable part of Canadian society. Although its effects have been devastating for individuals, the Kamloops Indian Residential School was not successful in its attempts to assimilate the Indigenous peoples of the central Interior of the province now known as British Columbia.

CHAPTER 3

School Life

Thus, at the inception of the Indian School question, we find
two main characteristics which have ever since continued, i.e.,
the principal of the per capita grant and the denominational
interest.

—UNSIGNED LETTER, BC ARCHIVES (ANONYMOUS 1908)

In recalling their time at the Kamloops Indian Residential School,
people shared memories that might be categorized in three ways:
general details of their daily lives, specific sensational incidents, and
their current impressions of what happened there based upon the
two former types of memories and their subsequent life experience.
The three types of memories intertwine with one another and, in so
doing, provide fascinating insights into the effects the school had.
Leo reported,

> To me, the Indian school, generally speaking, was sort of like
> you were taken over by a superior force, by the government, and
> [they] try to mould you into something else, and they were very
> strict about it.

Mildred had similar recollections:

At the Indian residential school, we were not allowed to speak our language; we weren't allowed to dance, sing, because they told us it was evil. It was evil for us to practise any of our cultural ways....

Some of the girls would get some Indian food.... They'd take it away from us and just to be mean, they'd destroy it right in front of us. You know, that's how bad it was.

Although there was some change over time, Indigenous culture was never accepted by the school as a real, living culture. Rather, it was seen as something archaic and undesirable, something to be annihilated. As the dominant culture gathered strength and perceived that Indigenous cultures were—in their view—dying, there was noticeable relaxation in what was allowed in the school. An examination of daily life accents these claims and demonstrates clearly the systematic destruction of culture that was attempted.

THE SCHOOL DAY

Morning came early for the students at KIRS in the 1930s.

In the morning, we had to get up at six o'clock, perfect silence. We all took turns going into the bathroom: we'd fill our basin full of water, and we'd take it to our bedside. We'd wash, take that basin, empty it, clean it out, put it back, fix our bed, get dressed, and as soon as you're finished—you only had half an hour to do all this—brush your teeth, get in a line, and stand in line in perfect silence. If you're caught ever speaking one word, boy, you got cuffed around.

And then we marched from there down to the chapel, and we spent over an hour in the chapel every morning, every blessed morning. And there they interrogated us on what it was all about being an Indian.... He would just get so carried away; he was punching away at that old altar rail ... to hammer it into our heads that we were not to think or act or speak like an Indian. And that we would go to hell and burn for eternity if we did not listen to their way of teaching. (Mildred)

What better way to work at indoctrination than to take hungry children early in the morning and subject them to a harangue on the evils of their family's way of life? It certainly appears to be a compelling way to create change. No attempt was made at dialogue or reaching a common understanding. The complete silence of the "objects" being addressed ensured there was little opportunity for the children to put this attack in a context that might enable them to more fully understand the words directed at them. They had no opportunity to question the priest and no opportunity to speak to one another about what they had heard. Those who were caught speaking to one another were quickly punished.

Oh, in church when the girls were laughing ... somebody must be watching. Just grab them by the neck, make them lay down on the floor till after church. (Minnie)

Of course, the Mass was given in Latin. Not only were the children expected to learn English, they were also exposed to a second incomprehensible language in church.

The KIRS chapel: "every morning, every blessed morning ..." |
Kamloops Museum and Archives, 6812

In later years, daily attendance at Mass was no longer mandatory. One of the benefits for those involved in sports or dancing was that they were occasionally excused from the daily chapel service. However, those who chose not to attend the voluntary services often found themselves assigned extra cleaning duties during the Mass time. Following chapel, the children again moved in ranks to the dining room. Staff ate in a separate room nearby. Eventually, a partition was constructed down the centre of the dining room so that the sexes could not view one another during meals.

Almost everyone interviewed mentioned the infamous porridge served every morning at KIRS. Prepared by students with only minimal supervision by the nuns or older students, it was described most often as lumpy and burnt. Josephine, who had been involved in preparing the porridge, described it this way:

> We had some pretty good cooks there and some pretty bad cooks.... When you make porridge in those great big pots ... you learned that porridge is to be cooked in boiling water and a bit of salt and that you stir it so that it doesn't burn on the bottom.... Well, if they cook it in just warm water and not boiling water, you can be sure it's going to be sticky because that porridge sits there all night.... If you have to, then you add a little more hot water in the morning. You know, that's one thing that sticks in my mind is this sticky porridge.

The porridge even became the focus of small gestures of resistance. Unfortunately, those who refused to eat it found it waiting for them at the next meal, as was the case with all rejected food. Others found the porridge a source of entertainment in an otherwise mundane morning meal.

> I used to get a kick out of that, when I think back. We used to have this habit [to see] who could stretch the porridge the longest. We'd take our spoon and we'd start tapping the porridge up and down. Finally we'd get it going like a long string of gum, and we'd see who could get it the longest. And we'd get caught and, boy, did we ever get a licking. (Mildred)

She went on to point out that the children usually ate it.

You know, when you're hungry, you'll eat anything. They put a blob of that [mush] in our plate, a piece of bread, a little bit of butter, and a glass of blue milk. (Mildred)

Meals were served by the children themselves, and at least one person felt there was some justification for the unappetizing food.

I forget how many kids there was when I was going there. Imagine trying to cook for them. You couldn't put [the food] into individual platters and make it look appetizing. You know, there had to be a big pot at the end of that table … [with] those eight children, eight on each side of the table, and one serves. (Josephine)

The dominant impression of mealtimes is a sense of regimentation. Individuality was not a goal for the teachers and supervisors here or at any other times. The large number of children who had to be fed were seen as objects to be processed as cheaply and efficiently as possible, then passed along to the next station.

Another source of concern to those interviewed was the inequity between the staff's food and the children's. Those who worked in the kitchen were most aware of the difference. One person suggested that the methods of preparation provided the greatest disparity. Rather than being cooked ahead of time in huge vats, the staff's meals were prepared just before serving. Others described in detail the tasty and nutritious food they saw being delivered to the staff dining room. Maria, who attended KIRS in the sixties, commented on the double standard which she felt was expressed in the inequity:

For them it was different.… They didn't eat the same food we ate; they ate much better food. We had mush, and they had bacon and eggs. They were separate from everybody else in one room where the whole staff ate.

This discrimination was mentioned by several people. The sense of injustice caused by the varying quality of the food was intensified when students saw the meals being taken into the staff room while they went in to their less satisfying meal.

Many people remember hunger. In his book *The Fourth World*, George Manuel names hunger as the first of three things that stand out in his mind about school. One of the participants in this study, Leo, reported,

> Something I remember was that I was always hungry. I lost weight there. I gained ten to twelve pounds in two months at home. I go down there and I lose two or three in ten months.

This child was, of course, growing. That some of his weight increase in summer was growth-related makes even more significant the subsequent loss during his time at school. During those ten months, Leo was actually losing weight at a time when he was still growing.

Following a less than satisfactory breakfast and morning cleaning duties, the children moved to the classroom block. For the new-comers, more adjustments were necessary for their introduction to another unknown.

> Our first day we went to the classroom. They had all these little desks lined up; I think there were about thirty or thirty-five seats in this little room, maybe more.... So this nun was there; she was our teacher. I still wasn't used to looking at these people.... We were going into this classroom two by two, and they just told us to sit down, so we got to pick any place. And some kids were

coming in that day [who] were really scared. The little girls were so scared they were crying really loud.... The girls were kicking and screaming, and two older students were holding them by the arms, trying to bring them in.... And that scared the rest of us, 'cause we were so small, sitting there wondering, "What's going on? Why are we here?" And day after day, we went back there, and it took us a long time to get to know each other. (Beverly)

The classroom: two hours a day until the 1940s. | *Kamloops Museum and Archives, 6608*

A child who started school at nine years of age remembered her awkwardness on that first day:

> You know when you first enter the room, you'd never seen desks before.... You were just like cattle. And these kids that were there ... were laughing at us, you know.... We were the same age, but they'd been in school before.... And they were our own people saying these things. (Anna)

The first hour of classroom time was devoted to religious train-ing. Although assimilation was the government's prime objective for Indian people, the Oblates' goal was "the development of a child's character in accordance with the true concept of Christian educa-tion" (Cronin 1960, 223). This concept as interpreted by teachers was of questionable worth to some of the students, in retrospect.

> I remember when we were in the school there that all other churches were wrong. If you believed or read any of the other books, you were going to hell. That was pushed into our brain day after day after day at school. Didn't matter what church, what religion ... the Catholic was the only church. There was no other church, absolutely. (Leo)

For others, religion became like any other class.

> It just started to be like arithmetic, like reading, being taught catechism while sitting in a row.... To me, anyways ... it didn't quite tie in because it went by the bell. It went by strict routine. I guess I missed the personal contact that we started with at home with Granny and with the priest.... And so it became like the main textbook was the catechism book, always memorizing ... the Baltimore Catechism. (Joe)

Happy Easter from KIRS. | *Kamloops Museum and Archives, 6275 PN6659*

Others recalled the sense of guilt they were expected to develop as a part of their training.

> When you're raised a Catholic, everything is wrong that you're doing. At least that was my opinion. If you went to the washroom, that was wrong. If you wiped your ass, that was wrong. If you looked at your private parts, that was wrong.... If you talked to this person, it was wrong, or if you looked at that person, it was wrong. The whole attitude of the religious upbringing really squashed you. You weren't able to express your true self. Everything was controlled. (Charlotte)

Some found that their developing religious sense shattered their image of self and family.

They started talking to us about sin, about what sin was.... I felt really dirty 'cause this [sexual abuse] happened to me.... They started teaching me their religion ... telling me who God was, what hell was, and what angels were.... They said, "Anybody that doesn't go to church is a pagan." I started thinking, "Hey, my parents don't go to church all the time. They must be pagans." ... People that got drunk, they would really put them down. I thought, "Gee, our family is really the pits." And I'd go home and I'd be really ashamed of my parents. (Beverly)

Although major celebrations such as First Communion and Confirmation were happy times—"Those were nice days because we got dressed up so nice, pretty dresses. Even the boys got special little clothes too" (Beverly)—the Sacrament of Penance, which preceded Holy Communion, was another matter.

They wanted us to go to confession and tell our sins. Well gee, I didn't know what kind of sin I was to tell. It was funny standing there in line on Saturday; we'd all be in the hall ready to go to confession. So we'd go into these little boxes, eh, and the priest would be in there, and one girl on the other side and one on this side, and it was dark.... The priest would say, "Okay, what did you do?" or whatever.... I used to make up lies and I'd say, "Oh, I told seventeen lies...." I just made up these things, and the priest would say, "Okay, I want you to go and say ten Hail Mary's, five Glory Be's and one Our Father" ... and we'd go do that. (Beverly)

For another student, confession became a time of great tension when the priest consistently asked her if she had had sexual relations with anyone. His unseemly interest in the subject, combined with his displays of affection for her, which involved touching her in public, led the student to believe that the priest was clearly making sexual overtures. In her family, displays of affection were minimal. Even if we assume the priest's intentions were harmless, his insensitivity to her discomfort was not.

The organized Catholic religion, a renowned force in early settlement in North America, had a profound effect on every student who attended KIRS. For those who had experienced an introduction to Catholicism before leaving home and whose parents had adopted and adapted the religion as part of their way of life, the cultural shock of its teachings had less impact. For others, the values enforced by the teachings of the religion, particularly the notions of evil, sin, guilt, and hellfire, were foreign and fearsome. The long-term effects of these teachings were many; in some cases, they are still being felt. The use of religion as a weapon in the attack on traditional Indigenous spirituality and other cultural aspects was particularly devastating to those individuals whose families were already struggling with the changes expected of them.

For many years of the school's existence, after the hour of religion each morning, a mere two hours were dedicated to academic subjects: basic reading, arithmetic, and writing, combined with a few other subject areas, such as art and social studies. Although some students felt comfortable with the expectations of them in the classroom, many others found the time threatening and unpleasant.

We were graded very much as we do today.... There were a lot of slow learners and then the ones that were a little better and then the ones that advanced quite fast and understand better than the others. I think I was about in the middle.

> For no reason, I think they said, "You have the brains; you're just lazy. We know you can do it." And I know I can do it, but oftentimes I got behind and then I stayed behind. (Josephine)

For this student, academic study became oppressive. She worked hard, but when she could not meet expectations and was told she was lazy, she felt totally inadequate. The teacher's comments were so different from her mother's gentle guidance to go and finish what was left undone. The extra severity of the teacher's verbal harangue undermined Josephine's desire to succeed. On the other hand, many people interviewed found time spent on the academic subjects to be relatively positive. They did find it difficult to recall specific details of the curriculum. When probed, the students had comments like this:

> I don't know what we learned. I remember we started learning, I think, Joe and Ruth books. We had readers.... I really can't even tell you what we learned. I remember this big book they used to have hanging on the front. It was something about Rover and Bob, and those were the words that we learned. And if we were really good with our work ... the teacher would go to the next pages of this great big book with big letters. I liked that. (Anna)

These students found the academic work challenging and their teachers fair. Regarding her teacher, Anna said,

> I thought she was quite fair. She had worked hard and she was a real teacher, you know. She really taught us....
>
> Oh, I know one of the first things we did.... She gave us papers and pencils and we had to write our name.... I was taught by someone to print my name with capital letters, and I could remember working on that. Oh, I was so proud that I could write my name.

Students' general comments about school are best summarized in the following quotation about learning the basics. Leo was the only one who mentioned work besides reading and arithmetic when discussing the elementary grades.

> You learned the three R's there—you know, the basics. You learned a little bit about history ... but there was no history about BC.... They never taught us why Vancouver was called Vancouver or anything like that. They taught us all about Quebec and French and all the explorers. We learned a bit about South America.... We learned about King Henry VIII and V and all those guys.

Needless to say, no Secwépemc history was taught. What with the ethnocentric bias of the times, only European-based history was deemed important enough to be taught in schools. Additionally, an effective tactic for dominating a nation or replacing it with an alternative way of life is to eliminate any reference to that group's historical presence and even contemporary contributions to the replacement society, especially in teaching the children.

A very significant aspect of education at the residential school is that, until the late 1940s, no child attended academic classes for longer than two hours a day. The discrepancy between the two hours of lessons in residential school and the five hours in public schools resulted in the inability of most residential school students to transfer into public school if they chose to continue their education after grade 8. In most cases, continuation was not encouraged and was considered inappropriate and unnecessary for Indigenous people. The governments and the missionaries had decided that Indigenous people should be farmers or farmers' wives, not scholars or professionals. A person who left school in the 1940s recalled,

I think once you left there, you're sixteen or seventeen, most of us. When I found out there was going to be no high school ... we didn't care about education anymore. We just wanted to work for a living....

[The priests] never talked to me at all. Never said, "How would you like to come back?" or "We'll make arrangements." ... Not like nowadays [when they] try to put you ahead.... You didn't have any counsellors, and the old folks didn't care one way or another. (Leo)

If Leo or any of the other students had decided to attempt high school or further education, they would have been breaking new ground with little support either from teachers at the residential school or from those at home.

Finally, in 1946, a very restricted high school program was instituted at the residential school. At that time, Joe Michel, a student from the Secwépemc Nation, began high school. The following year, five other carefully selected students, including Joe's future wife, Anna, joined him. For the first time in their lives, they were expected to attend school from nine to three.

Then came grade 9. We started high school and we had to go a full day ... and those teachers had to try and teach us to graduate in four years. We had to write provincial exams. (Anna)

In writing these provincial examinations, the students were judged alongside those who had been in the public school system for five hours a day for twelve years. The Secwépemc students had covered approximately five years' worth of public school during their initial eight years at KIRS. The fact that the six original graduates passed their exams with only the equivalent of nine years of public schooling demonstrated their superior academic ability. This comparison is not emphasized in existing accounts of the early graduates of Kamloops Indian Residential School. Was this a deliberate attempt to cover the inequities of the education system for KIRS students?

For scholarly students who were being encouraged by their teachers, academic studies were the high point of the day. These students tended to be the ones whose parents had explained to them that the purpose of going to school was to learn to read and write. The more able students frequently completed the three grade 1 levels—1c, 1b, and 1a—all in their first year at school.

> I did do all grade 1c, grade 1b, and grade 1a [which was] surprising [because] it took me so long to get started. I used to be so nervous about doing my work and wanting to do it so well. I actually punctured my book.... I put my pencil right through it—all that muscle tension—trying to get an A or B....
>
> [A] little past mid-year, I began to look at things, "I know this experience," ... and I got interested in matching it with a word that the teacher would have. And having this discovery, "Carrying water, I've done that." That's a simple experience that matched what I was doing. Making fire, that's a simple experience that matched with making fire in words. That drew me—this is exciting, this is fascinating ... just the mere fascination of matching a previous experience with the actual words. I would think of that after school and looking at a tree: "I must learn the word for tree. I must learn the word for mountain. I must learn the word for ground." (Joe)

This tremendous self-motivation led to success for this student.

For other students, general insensitivity to their concerns and those of their classmates made school time more tumultuous than it needed to be. Maria, who transferred to KIRS from the residential school in Williams Lake, was upset by an unexplained decision that she had to repeat a grade.

> I don't remember how they decided that I was to go back one more grade. I was grade 2 and they put me back in grade 1.... I remember thinking that it was negative, like maybe I was dumb or something like that. I don't remember being told why. They immediately put me back in grade 1. (Maria)

She now attributes this to bad record keeping on the school's part.

> The PR [public record] followed me to every school I went. It obliterated the fact that I went to residential school since I was six—with mistakes after mistakes. The record made it seem like I took the same modules three times. Maybe I did; I may have been too Tsilhqut'in with an accent and didn't learn my modules. What I would like to think is that I was too Tsilhqut'in for them.

The lack of any explanation demonstrates how the adults in charge failed to realize that the children were aware of and had serious concerns and questions about decisions being made regarding their lives. Anna reported suffering to this day because of action taken with a close friend from her reserve.

> The first few days of school, what I remember was Betty from our reserve was also a newcomer, and about four days after we came … all of a sudden, they packed her up and they sent her home. Why, I don't know, you know. And I think, "She's the same age as

me. We come from the same place. What's different?" ... I do not understand and I have feelings that somebody should explain it to me.... Why, who, and what made that decision? ... I don't know why ... but it hurts me today yet. (Anna)

Again a simple explanation might have sufficed to calm the child back then and throughout the years. Because Anna wanted to be at school, she worried that the same thing might happen to her: she might be taken away from it. She also worried for her friend and her feelings about having to leave school. Although this was characteristic of the treatment of children, before the 1960s particularly but even to the present day, the fact that the school personnel were serving both as teachers and as surrogate families to children from another culture might have indicated a need for special awareness of potentially upsetting situations. Even a simple explanation could have allayed some of the fears of the children involved. Perhaps a shortage of staff contributed to the inability of those involved to have the sensitivity to deal with the difficulties students encountered. Throughout the time of the residential schools and into the recent past, inadequate and inequitable funding for Indian education—a federal responsibility—has indicated the low priority given to Indian education in the governments' budgets and, more generally, in Canadians' concerns.

Memories of the lunch following morning classes were little better than those of the breakfast mush.

They used to put potatoes, turnips, carrots, chunks of meat, cabbage, everything, all in one pot and boil the hell out of it. By the time they were ready to serve it, you couldn't even see a little chunk of potato; it was all like a chowder. And that we had for lunch every day....

Fridays—I don't know where they used to go. Up Squilax somewhere, I guess, Adams River, and they'd get barrels and bar-rels of that spawned sockeye. They'd put them in barrels of salt, and that was what they cooked in great big pans. Then, [they'd] mash it ... and they'd blob it in our plate, and that was what we ate on Fridays: salty fish, always that blue milk. (Mildred)

Following lunch, the hard work of the day began. Accompanying the religious people's mission to Christianize was the government's goal to "civilize the Indians." The program for "civilization" included teaching students the skills required for farming, gardening, sewing, cooking, and cleaning. The result was beneficial to the residential school in two ways: government requirements were met, and the work necessary for maintaining the school was accomplished. In some years, the operation of the school actually showed a profit, and sums of money were sent to Provincial House in Vancouver. Leo, who several times made reference to his hunger at the school, shared this information:

We used to collect 300, 350 eggs a day from the chickens.... Now we got eggs every second Thursday, one egg apiece.... They must have sold the eggs.

In a 1954 report on KIRS, Father O'Grady wrote, "The finances are sound and a large surplus is sent annually to the Province" ("Acts of Visitation" 1943–1966, 29).

The sewing room: patching clothes and making underwear. | *Kamloops Museum and Archives, 6725*

Training in agriculture for the males and in household skills for the females was expected to create white people with brown skin: people who would meld into the larger European-dominated society or, at the very least, serve as farmworkers and maids for their households. All those interviewed talked of their memories of chores, usually in far greater detail than their memories of academic work. Not only did the work occupy considerably more time each day, it also occupied a greater portion of the students' consciousness about their lives in the school. The females' chores were clearly gender specific. "The afternoon is spent in the kitchen or the sewing room," reported one student who attended in the late thirties. Mildred, who attended earlier, recalled,

> I was mostly put in the dairy and in the sewing room, but there were a lot of other chores that each of us had.... We had to rotate our chores.... [In the sewing room], what we were doing was mostly patching clothes, and there was some things we had to make, like the underwear.

Over the years the amount of sewing done varied. One student described clothing made by cutting up army surplus uniforms and sewing them into tunics. In later years, most of the sewing was confined to patching.

Through rotation of the jobs, students experienced all aspects of housekeeping in order to become prepared for keeping their prospective homes in good European fashion. The contrast between the homes where the students' families lived and the residence buildings has already been mentioned. For many students who attended before mid-century, knowing how to wash and wax a floor was hardly appropriate preparation for life in a house with a dirt floor. Rather, the skills learned were designed to prompt students' dissatisfaction with their parents' way of life. Although no one could argue with the importance of developing better housing for some Indigenous peoples then and now, creating family disharmony and individual confusion about the inherent value of a waxed floor was another tactic in the culturally destructive plans of the residential school authorities and their bosses. Although those in control may have had little knowledge of Indigenous homes, always the European way was presented as the right and only way to live. Any other way of life was to be despised and changed.

When not occupied in the sewing room or with cleaning, the girls were on duty in the kitchen. Kitchen chores were described as follows:

> When you get into the kitchen, the cook assigned you. Some of them would be the cook's helper, some the pots and pans, and some the bowls and utensils. One was for the pantry; you sliced the bread and made sure you made enough for the meal and lunch in the afternoon. Then she would assign two girls to the dairy, where they churned the butter and made it into pounds. (Mildred)

Perhaps not surprisingly, the cleaning duties were shared by both the boys and the girls. Of course, they were required to remain segregated, with the girls on one side of the building cleaning their quarters and the boys on the other side cleaning theirs. Teams were assigned to the various areas.

> We had a change of office every month. Mother Superior would come down in an evening and ... she would read out names of who is going to work in the playroom ... cleaning the recreation room, the public bathrooms.... There was a group assigned to the chapel.... A group would go to the second floor—that's the classrooms, superiors' community. The halls had to be shined all the time. Then there was another group went upstairs to the dorm.... And then there was a group assigned to the laundry. (Mildred)

Joe reported similar duties and emphasized the familiarity of the teamwork involved.

We gradually got introduced to chores…. A cleanup team would be composed of some seniors, some intermediates, and some juniors … which was a good way…. At first maybe they were easy on us; we did the dusting. It was a lot similar to how I learned things at home, which was good.

We had the bathrooms to do. My job as a little one was to flush all the toilets or to pick up the big things so that the sweeper could sweep…. But I gradually got to know what the others were doing … we worked as a team…. There was enough time to get to know one another. I believe the term was one month at a time and then a new list was given.

The camaraderie that developed within the groups provided a welcome respite from the cultural attacks. As Indigenous children working together, they could divide the labour in what may have approached the familial way, with the older students acting in the role of parents, expecting the younger ones to help as they could and to gradually become aware of the more complex tasks to be done. In all likelihood, the reasons for the students' comfort with their work went unrecognized by supervisors. It is possible that the relative harmony with which cleaning was done was viewed by those in charge as confirmation that this kind of work was most suitable for Indigenous students. Through their apparent lack of knowledge of Secwépemc ways, the European overseers failed to appreciate that this work provided an opportunity for students to practise the traditional division of labour. A Secwépemc graduate of KIRS who later became a supervisor in the school found her approaches to chore supervision of the children different from those of the nuns who had guided her.

I found too if you treat them good and kind of make them like yourself, that you're not up there and they're down there, that they're easier to get along with, and you could get more out of them.... I worked with them a lot. I just didn't say, "You go in there and scrub the kitchen floor." I got down and I worked with them. (Josephine)

She attributed this ability to her mother's guidance.

I spent the first ten years with my mother.... I think she was my best teacher.... When we weeded, my mum weeded with us too. I remember her crawling beside us.

Throughout her years of doing school chores, the work she had done with her mother stood out as the best model. Cleaning time occupied a considerable portion of the day and, because it was a time when students could interact with one another to a certain extent and when supervision was necessarily less rigorous, most found it more relaxing than class time or prayer time.

While the girls were cooking and sewing, the boys gardened and farmed. Leo had this to say:

Oh, we learned a little about farming too. Not anything about fertilizer. They never explained to us why they do things. They just told us how to do it, you know, like harrowing, plowing, and seeding and planting potatoes.... When I got older, my last year or two, I used to do a lot of planting and irrigating in the garden.

They had huge gardens. And they had a planter where you put the seed in and you just follow in a straight line....

> And we learned a little bit about dairy, but we never learned
> anything about planning of anything, or the financing or account-
> ing or anything like that.

The last comment is coming from the perspective of a man who now understands considerably more about European business than he did, or was expected to, as a child. He recognizes now that as boys, they were being trained not to run a successful business as farmers, but simply to grow enough food to support their families and to provide a labour pool for neighbouring farms and ranches. Assimilation was stated as the goal of education for Indians, but the assimilation was to take place under conditions that would cause no threat to the surrounding business and farming community. The principle of ultimate control of labour and land resources by the cultural invaders in the guise of church and state was a powerful determinant of educational policy and practice.

The senior boys rose early to care for the livestock.

> The senior boys used to get up ... in the morning—those that go
> to the barn and milk the cows, feed the chickens, pigs—5:30 in the
> morning. You know, work over there an hour and a half. And then
> you'd come back and go to church for another pretty near an hour
> and then you'd have breakfast. (Leo)

Joe, who attended KIRS eight years later, reported that his work included the following:

> Dairy cattle, beef cattle, chickens, turkeys, horses, going haying....
> For a little while, we had pigeons, bees. Most of us made the sta-
> tions working through all of those places so we knew when it was
> our turn for planting.... We'd have a calendar and we'd mark off

the date when we planted, harvested, and how to test when they were ripe. Not too many of us used the apprenticeship. I suppose the skills were transferable.

"We learned a little bit about dairy ..." | *Archives Deschâtelets-NDC, Fonds Deschâtelets, St-Peter's photographies, Kamloops Residential School*

Although Joe never used the farming skills he learned at school, others did find the skills useful. Some of the boys also got involved with carpentry and shoe repair. These skills were taught as part of the technical school. Those who were selected to attend these classes avoided some of the chore detail, so they were pleased to be selected.

If you got into tech, it's nice and warm in the winter. And you learn how to do a bit of carpentry, the basic stuff, make joints and mortise.

One year, I was mending shoes. They had a lathe there and a couple of those shoelaps. They had great big pieces of real thick leather. We used to carve out soles and a heel ... tack it on and then you polish it. And running shoes, we used to sew thin black leather or patches. (Leo)

With their newly acquired carpentry skills, the boys were put to work maintaining the existing buildings, constructing a huge pig-pen, and installing a floor and ceiling in the new gymnasium.

The boys put in the flooring, finished flooring.... They used flat-head nails and they nailed it on the tongue so that the nailhead never showed. And we went over it after we finished. You couldn't see a hammer mark.... And we put in the Donnacona ceiling. We had to have high scaffolds, measure it out. We done that ourselves. So we learned a little. (Leo)

Leo eventually used these carpentry skills in building his own houses. The work done by the children was considered of prime impor-tance by government officials. As late as 1954, the Department of Indian Affairs Annual Report's description of the curriculum proudly listed the acquisition of these work-related skills as a part of the course of study for the majority of Indian children, particularly those "in less advanced areas" (Department of Citizenship and Immigration, Indian Affairs Branch 1956, 51).

For the church, the inculcation of Catholic values was of para-mount importance. At the bottom of the list of priorities for both parties was an introduction to basic reading, writing, and arithme-tic. The cultural invasion was clearly acknowledged, detailed, and documented. European ways are Canadian ways, and Indigenous people had to learn to comply with these expectations. One school official made this comment during the 1950s:

The problem of Indian education is not primarily one of giving the Indian children the same schooling as all our other children. It is a problem of changing the persevering Indian community into a Canadian community. Then the Indian child cannot help but grow up in a Canadian culture and then the ordinary Canadian school will meet their educational needs. (Mulvihill 1957, Tape 130-2)

The final part of the school day included an hour of study, supper, cleanup, some highly structured and closely supervised recreation time, more prayers, and then bed. Nighttime found the children cold, lonely, and frequently afraid. "At the Indian school, you only had one [blanket], no matter how cold it was" (Julie). The loneliness came with sleeping alone in a bed; many children had been accustomed to sleeping with siblings at home. The fear came with the unknown behind a closed door or with the nightly visits of the watchman.

We were not allowed to sleep with each other, and they were very strict about that. We were not allowed to talk to each other.... And at night, the watchman would come around, and we were very, very scared of him. We often thought he was wicked and ready to get us. I don't know where we got that idea from. (Maria)

One wonders along with Maria why the watchman was such a concern. The fear and loneliness often manifested in bedwetting. One person estimated that 25 percent of the boys wet their beds. A student who left in the 1960s remembered her bedwetting.

I never did do that when I was home. The first night ... when I peed the bed, I was so ashamed.... I was just filthy dirty. And I couldn't believe that I done it, you know. This is incredible.

I never wet the bed at home. Why am I doing it now? And I asked a thousand questions.

Always bedtime was the loneliest part of the day. The children longed for their parents, the warmth of the family bed, and the sense of security they had known.

EXTRACURRICULAR ACTIVITIES

In the late 1940s, numerous changes were made in the school. High school was introduced for a select few, and extracurricular activities such as competitive dancing, a brass band, and sports took on greater importance. Gradually, chore time was reduced as time for these other occupations assumed significance. It is possible that the presentation of KIRS student performances in public was seen as a positive public relations move by the school's administration, as Gresko has claimed about another boarding school (1986, 96). Work was in progress on revisions to the Indian Act, and both politicians and school officials were conscious of the fact that the schools, which had been meant to make "Indians" disappear, had not been successful.

Some students found their successes in various fields rewarding. Sam commented that the KIRS teams "were the best at everything: soccer, basketball, everything." The benefits of being on teams were not limited to winning at sport. Many people felt that simply getting away from the school was a major attraction of participation. At the same time, interviewees were justly proud of their achievements while involved in the various sports. One man described his success at boxing. He qualified to fight in the Buckskin Gloves tournament three years running. The ultimate tournament of the year, it required that boys place in the six or seven prior tournaments held throughout the region. Only the top four or five boxers from each region were selected, and qualifying to box at even the smaller meets was no mean feat. Sam said,

> The only outside activity was sports. In order to go and compete anywhere outside, you had to beat out two hundred other people. Maybe that's why you were the best out there. Even in boxing you had sixty or seventy other people to beat out each year. So you weren't sparring, you were boxing.

Starting in the late 1940s, extracurriculars provided some respite. | *Kamloops Museum and Archives, 7905*

"You weren't sparring, you were boxing." | *Archives Deschâtelets-NDC, Fonds Deschâtelets, St-Peter's photographies, Kamloops Residential School*

Archie, who left the school in 1959, spoke highly of the school, largely as a result of his association with team sports. He too had felt a keen sense of competition.

> If you stubbed your toe, they just put someone else on. So you had to give 100 percent.... You had to work hard to make the team....
>
> We got to play for the teams in town. That was what was really enjoyable about this school. The intermediate teams in town drafted students from this school to play. We even got to stay at the coach's house on the weekends.

The disciplinarians may even have seen that fostering a sense of competition among the boys had some spinoff benefits for the control of the students, through something of a divide and rule philosophy.

Traditionally, Secwépemc communities survived through families cooperating with one another. One former student who was very successful in sports found that it noticeably strained his relationship with his less successful brothers. As a result of the competition fostered between them at school, they have never been close.

The administration's recognition that the school's public image was enhanced through the children's success in competition also played a role in the development of competitive dance groups in the school. Dance groups were seen by many students as a source of variety in their lives, especially with travel to competitions. Dancers also recognized the special benefits available to them.

> The only reason why I stayed in the dance group was because you got privileges.... Sometimes on Sunday, you didn't have to get up for early Mass. Then you sometimes got extra goodies that other kids didn't get.
>
> I really enjoyed myself when we went to Revelstoke on the train. I thought that was pretty neat.... My mum had bought me this really nice hat and dress outfit. (Julie)

Beverly had hoped that joining the dance group would help her stay out of trouble.

> I said, "Well, if I have to stay here, I might as well get something out of this place." So I decided to join their dancing group.... They let me join, I don't know why. You know, I didn't even know if they would take me after running away.

Membership in the dance group was viewed as prestigious. Although the training was rigorous, many girls enjoyed the opportunity to feel good about themselves and revelled in the admiration of outsiders. It is notable that although the dance group performed dances from many European countries, such as the four- and eight-hand reel, Irish jigs, and the Swedish masquerade, no Secwépemc dances were performed. Even up to the final days of the school, the Secwépemc culture was not recognized as a legitimate one worthy of recognition.

A member of the drum and bugle band. | *Kamloops Museum and Archives, Jack Kelly Fonds, News Photos file 10–Indians #1970.073.010.006*

Fancy costumes and "unusual" headdresses for the drum and bugle band. | *Kamloops Museum and Archives, 7137*

Although members of the drum and bugle band wore "unusual" headdresses, and students were eventually permitted to "Indian dance" for fun, activities generally continued to be fashioned on the European model.

Not all was pleasant for the girls who decided to become dancers. Julie, a long-standing member of the group, had some particularly bitter memories.

My toenails are permanently damaged from [having] to stand on your toes. If you didn't stand on your toes, you were whacked with a ... shillelagh, and she'd whack you damn hard on your legs....

The first few times you really tried because you found out that things were a lot better if you were a dancer.... You went places too, so that made you want to get out of that school.

But then after a while, it's not fun anymore; it's a chore because you're never any good.... They never swore at you but they called you dumb and stupid ... and so then the fun was out of it. And after a while you kind of didn't want to do it, but ... they didn't want to retrain somebody, so they'd keep making you do it.

I remember the first time I ever got whacked. I stood there and thought, "Well, I'm going to defy this woman." ... I just glared at her and she gave me another one and I kind of glared. But I wasn't glaring too hard 'cause it hurted, and the next time she whacked me, I really broke down and howled.

Even the prizes began to lose their meaning for Julie: "You won prizes and wondered why the hell you even bothered to go, because when you got back it was still the same way."

Charlotte, who observed the dance training, also remembered the stick and the successes.

If you were dancing, she'd come up and she'd hit you on the legs, "Lift them legs up!" Geez, them poor girls would be just a ... you know. They learned those Scottish jigs, the different types of dances from the different parts of the world. But the girls really won a lot of medals for it, so it was good encouragement for them.

While offering some encouragement to the girls, the main purpose of the dance groups were as showpieces to be displayed in public for the school's prestige and to create public support for the work of the church. The relevance of the dances to the students' lives and the long-term benefits of the rather savage training are highly questionable. With little connection to the Secwépemc culture, they appeared to be merely someone's idea of what would be good for "them," the Indigenous children of KIRS.

The Mexican troupe, ca. 1962. Dance troupes served as public showpieces for KIRS. | *Kamloops Museum and Archives, 6276, PN6660*

As noted earlier, in the fifties, a rare few deemed to have exceptional academic ability participated in semi-private extracurricular discussions with stimulating instructors. For those students, the time was a welcome relief from the impersonal atmosphere of much of the rest of the day. Some of the lessons dealt with a more philosophical view of both religion and the academic subjects.

Some priests here would call a few of us into a dialogue of life.... They called us in a room, and they would just give us the freedom to explore different things of life and tie some things together.

Another one ... used to take some of us to have discussions about history and almost philosophical areas.... His get-togethers

with us were much like a university seminar. And he'd just challenge us ... he would give us time, "You think of that, close your
eyes, extend." He would say, "There is a university. There are thousands of books on this. Your mind can keep on going."

They taught me more about looking at things than the classroom 'cause the classroom was mundane. These were idea things,
and he respected our ideas, no matter how small they were. (Joe)

The group described met during the forties and consisted of five or
six boys out of a school population of 300 to 350. Although these
lessons were highly stimulating for those few, many of whom went
on to become chiefs and leaders, they were not considered appropriate or wise for the vast majority of children. This kind of careful
selection and enrichment of a chosen few is typical of the hierarchical system that is part of all aspects of European society, including
the organized church. It appears to have been an attempt to induct
these particular children into the belief system that a special few are
entitled to privileges unfit for the general population.

Although clearly not part of the intent, the meetings also provided opportunity for the children involved to experience a setting
more like their home environment and to reinforce Secwépemc
ways of relating to children respectfully. A notable aspect of Joe's
comment is "He would give us time." In recent studies of Indigenous
learning styles, the amount of time between asking a question and
expecting an answer has proven very significant. Many Indigenous
students, like many non-Indigenous ones, respond with much more
regularity and depth when they are given adequate time for thought
before responding. If this approach had been used in the regular

classrooms, what would the effect have been for student engagement and success at the secondary level?

Junior girls wait their turn to visit the museum, October 15, 1939. | *Kamloops Museum and Archives, 973*

Other happy memories centre on general recreation time, special holidays, outings to town, and general changes for the better. Trips to the museum and to the local theatre were special treats. Though they marched in regimented lines, the students at least had the opportunity to move out of the endless routines of school and work. One student commented specifically on the good times she remembered.

It wasn't all bad. We had a lot of fun. We looked forward to the picnics, Christmas.... We stayed here for Christmas so we used to have little concerts ... it made us feel good.... It was just a real treat to have a bought doll. I got one.... Every one of the kids had a bought gift for the first time in our whole life. That was the highlight of my school days. (Sophie)

Changes in the late forties were attributed to a new principal arriving at the school.

And then they began buying us beads. We were able to string beads and make little beaded things.... We had a radio for the playroom.... Then the priest allowed us to have dances—just girls, no boys ... Friday night.... We were allowed to wear clothes from home.... We began to get nicer food.

Junior girls view exhibits, October 15, 1939. | *Kamloops Museum and Archives, 974*

Marching to the drum, the boys go the movies. | *Kamloops Museum and Archives, 6854*

Minnie, who attended near the turn of the century, fondly remembered a picnic.

> Gee, one time, the sister and that man that looks after them, we went up straight over the mountain. We got some lunch. After we got over, way down there's a creek ... we picnic (they call them picnic).

The opportunity to be in an environment more like home, particularly like the fondly remembered summer camps, must have felt good to this little girl. Beverly, who attended much later, during the sixties, reminisced about her recreation time.

> In the rec room … they used to have a radio there. We used to
> listen to the songs … Elvis Presley…. I used to like his songs…. I
> don't know how I started learning to dance…. This one supervi-
> sor we had, she said, "Do you know what? I wished I was a good
> dancer." She was an Indian lady that they hired…. I said, "I think
> I know how to dance," … so she got her record player and she put
> a record on, and I and her started to dance…. All the other little
> girls used to watch…. Then I started teaching them how to dance,
> and after that everybody danced.
>
> We played baseball and sometimes … we'd sit around and we'd
> make up stories…. "Boy, if I was rich, I would do this and that,"
> you know.

The presence of a Secwépemc person as supervisor, while not
changing the system, did make a difference to some aspects of the
children's daily lives. With her, the children could feel some connection to home and probably had an opportunity for reinforcement
of some cultural patterns. Beverly felt comfortable enough with the
Secwépemc supervisor to take a leadership role at recreation time.
She also commented on her fantasies of being rich.

> I don't know how we were exposed to richness and happiness….
> When we got to intermediate, it was a little harder. 'Cause then
> some of the kids there were a little richer…. You get to wear your
> own clothes … you're allowed to fix your hair…. If you were poor,
> you didn't have anything nice…. It was a hard time because of the
> peer pressure. (Beverly)

Peer pressure can be particularly debilitating when children are
exposed to it twenty-four hours a day. For children who are with

their families, the pressure is usually limited to school hours, but in the residential school, there was no escape. In this case, as with the dance group, the happy times were tainted with some painful memories.

Beverly also spoke negatively of recreation time. A particular priest was the cause of her concern.

> That one priest, he was kind of odd ... I was kind of scared of him, I guess.... We were at the movie there one Friday night. He went and he sat with the little girls. I was kind of watching, and I said, "Gee, it must be nice to have a friend." Anyway, I ended up beside him ... and all of a sudden he started to feel my legs.... I was getting really uncomfortable and he started trying to put his hands in my pants.... And I just got up and I moved right away, but I never thought to tell anybody.

A number of people mentioned sexual overtures made to them during their time at school. This priest was also said to spend extensive time around the little girls when they played outside. This kind of abuse of the children moved beyond acting on racist beliefs to sexual assault.

In a much lighter vein, one student recollected an incident connected to Indian dancing at the school. This was the only time the people interviewed mentioned what could have been traditional Indigenous dancing. Significantly, by this time in the late fifties, religious and political pressures had exerted enough influence that people in power were confident—wrongly, of course—that Secwépemc culture was rapidly disappearing. For this reason, some dancing could be allowed without jeopardizing their intent of bringing Secwépemc people into mainstream European-influenced society. As a new older student coming to the school for the first time, Charlotte was challenged by other students to show her "Indianness." In response to a nun's inquiry as to who knew how to "Indian dance,"

> One of those two hollered out, "Charlotte knows how to Indian dance," and I didn't.... So Sister says, "Okay, get up there and dance." And I thought, "Oh my God, I don't know what the heck I'm doing." And I thought the only person that's going to know the mistake ... are the girls themselves because they're Indian. Sister ain't going to know, so she ain't going to hit me on the legs.... I got up there and just did a war whoop and dance, just really faked it.

With that performance, the new girl passed the test put to her and was accepted by the other students.

Most noteworthy about all of these extracurricular activities is that they provided a respite from the regimented day. They also provided an opportunity for some students to grow in confidence and self-esteem. While the existence of Secwépemc culture was still predominantly denied, extracurriculars did serve in some cases as a successful foundation upon which the students could build. At the least, the recreational activities gave students a chance to relax, to get to know one another, to remember and practise some culturally related behaviours, and to dream a little of what might be.

KIRS girl cadets parade to the cenotaph, November 11, 1958. |
Kamloops Museum and Archives, R.B.A. Cragg fonds
#1989.009.050, #1 June 20, 1948–July 27, 1960 slide 150

The Indian School parade float: from classroom to basketball court. |
Kamloops Museum and Archives, Jack Kelly fonds, News Photos
file 10–Indians, Photo #1970.073.010.032

DISCIPLINE

Discipline in the Kamloops Indian Residential School was severe. Based perhaps on the old saying "Spare the rod and spoil the child," punishment was a topic the former students raised repeatedly. Most often they remembered the strap, but other forms of punishment, including public humiliation, head shaving, and bread and water diets, were also reported. Minnie, the oldest person interviewed, recollected, "Some people got punished; they got to lay down on the floor. Just pure bread and water to eat, laying on the floor … oh, I don't know how many days." Mildred brought to mind these scenes.

> I was punished quite a bit because I spoke my language…. I was put in a corner and punished and sometimes, I was just given bread and water…. Or they'd try to embarrass us and they'd put us in front of the whole class.

Public humiliation was one of the worst forms of punishment for the children. Traditionally, the possibility of other people laughing at a person served as a strong social control. James Teit, in his extensive anthropological study of the Shuswap, recounts lists of taboo behaviours, almost all of which include the warnings that those who do such things will be laughed at or gossiped about. To add insult to injury, the strap was frequently administered publicly.

> If we got caught, we really got punished, and if that didn't work, we got sent to the principal's office. And that was lashes we got there, in front of the whole school: real humiliation. (Mildred)

Maria, a Tsilhqut'in student who attended in the sixties, recalled,

I got in trouble for chewing gum.... It was such a minor, minor thing in my view. But I was taken into the playroom.... She was a layperson. She took down my pants right in front of everybody.... Can't remember whether she used her hand to spank me or whether she used a ruler or a strap ... but I remember being punished.

Josephine, who attended much earlier, remembered the worst strapping she ever received because of its injustice.

One time, we were issued these barrettes.... You only got one a year.... One of the intermediates had lost hers, so she said, "Can you lend it to me until right after the check?" ... It was the very time that sister noticed I didn't have it on.... I got the strap for that.... I didn't want to tell on the girl either, so I got punished.

She remembers there were a "lot of strappings going on.... They took your pants down and they lean you over a bench in front of everybody." Again public humiliation was combined with corporal punishment. Perhaps the punishers understood enough of Secwépemc culture to know that public humiliation was the worst form of punishment, or perhaps a lack of awareness caused them to punish children doubly. In either case, the punishments used, although most often effective, appear inhumane in retrospect.

Bedwetters were also punished severely.

When I was a junior, I used to wet the bed—whipped us for that too. He had a scheme; he tried to stop people from wetting the bed.... First of all he tried to get us up a couple of times at night.... For a lot of us it didn't work, so he thought he'd do it the hard way,

> give them whippings.... He finally quit doing it. That was on your
> bare [bottom] too. (Leo)

Other children remembered having their wet sheets put over their heads and then being spanked. One admitted, "I don't remember that part, or I don't want to remember" (Mildred). Such memories were too painful to live with and were repressed. A man recalled that the little boys had to wash their sheets in the river and that his daughter had been locked in a cupboard for continual wetting of her bed (field notes). Several others mentioned washing their own sheets every day. Bedwetting, so frequently a manifestation of children who are upset in some way, was a sure sign that life was very stressful for many children at KIRS.

Head shaving was another form of punishment actually considered more severe than strapping, perhaps because of the traditional associations already mentioned. The initial haircut was punishment enough. Shaving was worse.

> As a little girl, my hair was really long and curly.... My hair was
> down to my hips.... Sister cut it; she kept cutting it till she shaved
> my hair 'cause she thought I was curling my hair.... It was very evil
> for us to have curly hair. Everything we did was evil. (Mildred)

A runaway in the early sixties, Beverly retraced these painful steps:

> When I got back to the school, because I ran away, they were
> going to give me punishment. So instead of strapping me, they
> said, "You got to kneel down on the floor in front of everybody
> and tell them you're sorry you ran away...." Because I ran away,
> they said they were going to give me a real short haircut for pun-
> ishment. So my hair was cut really short, almost like a boy's.

By this time, the disciplinarians must have recognized that public mortification was the worst form of chastisement for the children and that head shaving was effective in that it created long-term easily recognized disgrace.

Other physically abusive disciplinary action was also mentioned. One brother who looked after the first aid post provided this gruesome treatment to Leo when he scratched the sore on top of his head.

> He had a pitcher there, and he used to always have castor oil in it. When he got mad at somebody ... he'd take that castor oil and grab him by the hair and fill his mouth up.... I must have been about seven or eight years old then. He pulled my head back and he filled my mouth with castor oil and pretty near made me gag. Then he kept my head back till I swallowed it.

This treatment was nothing short of cruel and unusual punishment inflicted by a short-tempered person. It is not known whether the action was common or not, but the constant presence of the jug suggests perhaps it was. Another episode of cruelty involved a little boy who was hungry.

> One thing that sticks in my mind was the one little guy.... Poor little thing, I guess he was so hungry, he used to go down to the river bank and pick those thorn berries.... One day he filled all his little pockets ... and the darn principal, he was so mean. He grabbed that little boy and turned him upside down by his legs and shook him. Berries went all over the floor. The little boy stood there crying. All these humiliating things that they did to us. (Mildred)

Although the students suffered numerous mistreatments such as these, little could be done about them. Until the fifties, students were in residence eleven months out of the year. Letters written home were always censored. Leo reported the following:

> They censored all our letters. If you made a complaint ... they would make a big speech—if we complained about food in a letter. There wasn't very many that complained ... 'cause we knew it wouldn't get out anyway.

Julie wrote to her grandmother to ask if she could live with her instead of staying at the school.

> I never did ever get an answer from her.... I didn't know that the nuns never sent the letter 'cause they read [it].... They'd censor your letters and so they never bothered sending my letter.

Punishment as a form of training was an integral part of the work of the children's keepers. Children were to learn to be obedient, to abandon their Indigenous cultures, and to comply with regulations. Perceived or deliberate lack of cooperation was dealt with quickly and firmly. One could assume that under the circumstances—many children and few staff—these measures were seen to be expedient. The appropriateness of the castigations and the long-term effects are more questionable. While corporal punishment was at that time an accepted part of European Canadian culture, for the Secwépemc children, such punishments must have been incredibly harsh.

FAMILY VISITS AND SUMMER HOLIDAYS

Family visits and summer holidays created a myriad of complex emotions for the children at KIRS. Although remembered with mixed feelings, contact with family provided some continuity and support for the students and left them with the feeling that, while school might seem inescapable, outside its walls, Secwépemc life carried on. Ultimately such interactions may be seen as positive; at the time, the children felt torn. During the interviews, there were a number of common responses expressed; in some cases, the feelings were specific to individual circumstances. For those whose families saw value in adaptation to some European ways, such as learning to read and write in English, the children had a sense of continuing— though disrupted—family relations. On the other hand, children whose parents could not or did not confide in them about the purposes and the limitations of their time in school were the most affected by its assault on their understandings of themselves, their families, and their cultures. A sense of confusion and even betrayal infiltrated their thoughts.

A commonly mentioned reaction to parents was one of anger and a feeling of rejection for being sent to the school. For these children, family visits tended to reinforce the confusions.

We were there from August; we only had one month's summer holiday, and that was July…. We never even went home for Christmas, and we were allowed parent visits only about once a month….

In time they come; you got used to it, [the school]…. You were torn in between…. I know I blamed my parents for putting me there because I felt they didn't want me. And I blamed the sisters and the fathers that they were trying to take something away from me…. I felt I was beginning to have hate…. I was beginning to have resentment against my mother and my dad because I felt …

that they didn't love me, that they just put me in there and threw me to the wolves. (Mildred)

Family visit to Easter concert, ca. 1930. | *Kamloops Museum and Archives, 1874*

Mildred recalled the pain of exerting tremendous self-control when her mother visited.

I remember they came once in the fall and just for a little while.... They came in the truck, and I went with them in the truck just a little ways. We sat and we talked and it felt really different.... There are no tears or anything because I understood what is going to happen for a few years. But I think if I was younger I might have been clawing her and scratching her. But I'm a young lady, eh, and I know why. It was nice she came.

The final comment demonstrates the importance of Mildred's mother's visit, despite her internal ambivalence. Although some of the feelings of disappointment may be attributed to the children's unfulfilled expectations of family visits, just below the surface was the dashed hope that somehow the visit would save them from the oppressive system, that miraculously they would be able to go home and be a part of the family again. Clearly, the children found school an unhappy and challenging place to be, even those whose parents had carefully told them why they were there.

In contrast, Archie, who attended in the 1950s, found that the regular biweekly visits of a mentor-uncle were of great significance to his survival and having positive moments at the school. This uncle, who took Archie away from the school during his visits, offered advice and encouragement, suggesting ways to make the most of his school experience. The uncle's unfailing interest, particularly in Archie's participation in team sports, was a great support and also helped him to develop a keen sense of competition that has served him well in his rodeo career.

For some people whose parents were far away or busy with a large family at home, visits were impossible. Josephine said,

Some kids had parents that came all the time, but ... where we live way up here ... you had to catch the train.... I think once [when] we were at the school they travelled way down to go to work in the tomato fields; they travelled down with their horse and wagon. And money was hard to come by so we didn't get anything. We never come home at Christmas. A lot of children did, but as I grew older, I thought that was just it because there we had the whole school, and everything was just relaxed.

Over time, Josephine grew accustomed to school and accustomed to seeing little of her parents during the school year. Her distance from the family's way of life also grew.

Although some parents took their children away from the school during visits, many interviewees described rather stiff meetings in the school parlour, with the principal frequently hovering nearby. These visits were one of the few occasions that siblings of different ages and sexes were permitted to be together. Beverly recounted,

> I can't remember what holiday it was, but my parents came to visit.... I was really happy to see them. I wanted to go home right away but my mum ... said that I couldn't go home. It was really hard to see them leave us.
>
> We met in this one room they called the parlour, and there was a few benches in the room.... The priest would come around to the door once in a while, and the principal would say hello.
>
> I didn't know why I had to stay, why they couldn't say I could go home with them, because I thought, "Well, they're my mum and dad. They used to decide whether I could go home with them or not." Before I went there, they used to leave us with sitters, and they'd come and pick us up. I couldn't understand why they couldn't just say, "Okay, let's go home."

While the connections between family members during these visits were clearly important in maintaining a kind of family unity and a sense of culture of origin, the pain of the inevitable separation that followed was excruciating. In terms of the plan to have students become a part of Euro-Canadian culture, school personnel may have found the visits somewhat of a detriment in that they reminded the child who they were and who their family was. In the maintenance of the child's sense of being Secwépemc, being part of a family, the visits were integral.

Holidays raised similar turmoil in the students' minds. Adjustment periods were common when students arrived home. Julie remembered her siblings' return.

> [They] would come home from that school and they weren't running around and being themselves. They were quiet and sometimes just sat for hours.... My younger brother and I were just [thinking], "Oh, these guys are really bloopers: they just sit and do nothing."
>
> Mum would say, "You kids, get out there and feed the chickens," and John or Rosie would say, "That's not my job."
>
> By then, they were defying Mum.... They got so they had to get lickings to get them to go do things.

For the whole family, adjustments were necessary. The children felt out of place and had begun to assume behaviours and respond only to treatment common to residential school. Rather than recognizing that duties were shared by the family, they began to defy their parents and await punishment as a means of enforcing requests.

Language was another area of concern. For some the transition back to their native language was smooth. As time went on, though, more parents spoke only English due to their own training at the residential school—training which convinced them that their language had no place in Euro-Canadian society—and as a result of increasing involvement with English speakers, both Indigenous and non-Indigenous. Joe said,

When I learned my Shuswap, we lived as a total family unit. Previous to 1938, there was not much moving about outside of the reserve area.... When I came to school ... I can see now my father began branching out working away from home; my grandfather went farther away from home.... The Shuswap language continued to be spoken whenever [the family] got together, but as we gained more knowledge of the English and because of ranching out, [work] in logging camps, they moved gradually to speak more English. And then when we all came home, I could see the switch into English as we started to move through the years.

They would slip into Shuswap whenever an Elder would come who had not left the reserve, and they would just flick back and forth in that way.... That happened in our family, and I think that happened in a large number of other families.

This statement summarizes very clearly the erosion of the language that occurred in the Secwépemc territory and beyond. By the last few years of the school's operation, almost all students coming to school had prior knowledge of English, and in some cases, they had never learned their own language. Those who had suffered for speaking Indigenous languages wanted to help their children avoid similar punishment.

For some students going home just felt good. Anna remembered,

We were poor, eh, and I don't know why going home was so good. Because love is what covers it all. And then you're free to talk, and you're just right back, and it's all open, open door again.... For the first few days, we were speaking English, and then after a while we started mixing it. And then by end of summer we were speaking Shuswap again.

Leo had similar feelings. He acknowledged that although

> it wasn't as clean ... I was happier at home.... I know I get lots
> to eat and I get a bit of free time.... I could play. I had to work
> sometimes making hay and weeding the garden, but I was just as
> happy to be home. When we had our chores done, we could roam
> the country. Do as we wish.

The plentiful food supply of summer and the contrast to the oppressive system of the school stood out in most students' minds. At the same time, their memories emphasize the authoritarian nature of school. When children prefer making hay and weeding gardens to school life, one must assume that the school's tasks are more arduous and less relevant to good relations within family. In the final analysis, home visits were essential to maintaining a sense of self, family, and culture distinct from the residential school.

For some children in the later years, going home became a time of disappointment. The reality of a family and a culture being eroded by the pressures of an increasingly domineering European influence was not pleasant.

> Because we were then all through the system, we clung together,
> you know, like just us kids. And Mum and Dad were kind of
> out.... By then they'd started drinking. See, when we first started
> going to that school, they never drank.... I guess because there
> was none of us kids at home, they started drinking, so when we
> came home, it was something different. I mean there was booze
> in the house, there was parties, and things started really changing
> from what we knew of it before.... (Julie)

One can only imagine the impact and the sorrow when parents had their children taken from them; alcohol was one way to ease their sense of loss. Beverly felt a personal sense of shame at her parents' drinking: "I thought, 'Wow, these guys are drunks,' and it was like I didn't have a place anywhere—not at the school and not at home."

Maria recalled her homecoming as follows:

> Upon arriving home, we would be really excited ... and then there would be a drunk Daddy, Mum not feeling so very good, and that would bring down the whole excitement. You'd be disappointed, but you would be glad to see your parents.
>
> After like a day or so, we would be back into playing outside, looking at the old playgrounds ... and spending some time with Mum in bed, with her telling stories.
>
> I remember as I got older when I went home, I found it hard to speak our language to my parents.... I remember stumbling, stumbling, stumbling, and the words not coming fluently, so I think we were rusty for quite a while.

Home visits then conjured up a sense of happiness too often accompanied by a growing sense that life had changed irrevocably. This change was not simply the gradual one of a child growing older. Consciously and subconsciously, the children recognized that the culture which defined them and their parents was not acceptable to the dominant society around them.

Summers ended, and the children returned to school. Julie spoke of the bittersweet memories of the last days.

> Before we'd go back to school, we'd go bring the cows in.... We'd stay out in the bloody mountains and just thoroughly enjoy

ourselves.... It would be just about like how it was before but, you know, you'd never ever get back to it because ... you got a lot of hurts for feelings and you know what's ahead of you.

The impossibility of living as a family on a continuous basis and the understanding that life would never be as it was are clearly stated. Anna, who said she actually enjoyed school, remembered her first days back after the holidays.

I knew I couldn't stay home. I knew that. But the times that really, really gets to the bottom of my soul: the first day back.... You're feeling pretty lonesome, suddenly go to bed, and in the morning, you wake up and you see this white ceiling. You may as well have a knife and stab me through my heart. You know where you are, and you got to survive, and you just cover it over, seal it up for ten months.

Anna's attempt to seal up her real self for ten months in order to survive the oppressive system was one way of protecting her identity as a family member and a Secwépemc person. With the return to school, the attack on familial ways of life was renewed. This time the students knew what the system held for them and found little solace in that knowledge.

One must face the inevitable question of why parents sent their children to KIRS. For some, there was an understanding that learning to read and write English was of paramount importance. The Oblates did a good job of convincing people that parochial school was the most effective place for learning the catechism. And the Department of Indian Affairs included a clause in the Indian Act stating that attendance was mandatory; failure to comply carried fines and threats of imprisonment or other penalties.

Mildred attended the school herself and wanted to keep her own children out. She reported the following:

> With the experience I had as a child, I did not want to see my children being given the abuse I had.... When we first sent our children to the public school, we fought the system.... The Department of Indian Affairs went as far as saying we'd lose our status.... They said we'd have to pay for our children's education. We said we would because we didn't want our children to suffer the way we did.
>
> The Oblates told us we'd go to hell. They really sort of discriminated against us.... They told us that the white man's teaching would corrupt the children's minds.

In the face of this opposition, this family finally relented and sent their children to the residential school as day pupils. Other parents recognized the power of the dominant society and hoped that school could ensure an equal position for their children.

> I don't ever remember any of my grandfather or mother telling me about the nature, about the culture of Indians. They never spoke about the Indian culture, and I think they already were starting to forget, even as old as they were. They seen a white man ... in a better world, so they didn't stress our culture.... There was a few things they would teach you. (Leo)

Leo also told extensive stories about details of Secwépemc culture, including eating Indigenous food from the wild. Important to note are his feelings about his parents' thoughts. He had internalized the message that European ways were superior to Secwépemc ways. Maria, who attended years later, reported that her father thought the whites "were the smartest human beings on earth."

There were other, more practical reasons parents sent their children to residential school. Leo, in reference to his foster parents, recounted,

> They send the kids so they don't have to feed them in the winter. You know, these are the facts of life. You can't deny it.... Big families didn't have enough to feed some.

Years later, Sam, who transferred back into KIRS after spending some time in public school, explained, "The only reason I was able to go to school in town was because I stayed home with Mum. If they could support you at home, then you could go." Later, when no one at home was working, residential school became a necessity, as his mother found it impossible to provide for the children. Julie, in retrospect, understood her mother's unspoken reasons.

> It was just what she figured was best for us. Like she wanted us to learn the white man's way so we'd get ahead in the world. And here we thought she hated us.

Many children did not attend. Some came late, at the age of nine or ten. Many left early, when they became sick, and never returned. Minnie said,

> The priest sends me home. I'm always sick. I don't stay. Go to school every day—earache, sore throat, oh, all kinds of sickness. So the priest send me home. He told me, "I'll talk to the people to come down for you and they take you home—no use to stay here."

Mildred, another student, reported,

> The only way I got out was I was very sick. So my father and
> mother went to Indian Affairs and told them. I had scarlet fever
> then ... I got out ... and I only had grade 3.

Neither of these two ever returned to school. One person I spoke
with recounted that his parents took him home from school after a
sibling was killed in an accident at home, and they wanted to have
him close to them (field notes). Some children ran away and were
well hidden. Some did not find their names on the list in the fall.
One child who sincerely wanted to attend because she saw all the
others going to school was kept home to do chores for an aging
grandmother (field notes).

Those parents who did send their children did so for one or
more reasons: they recognized the importance of literacy; they were
respectful of the church's wishes; they believed that European ways
were superior; or they found it difficult to feed their families because
their traditional hunting and food gathering lands were occupied by
the settlers (viz. Redford 1979–1980). As time went on, more parents kept their children home either to attend one of the growing
number of day schools established on reserves or to go to public
school. Others who lived close to the residential school decided to
send their children as day pupils when this choice became possible.

Students and staff at KIRS, with acrobats completing the picture, n.d. | *Kamloops Museum and Archives, 8015*

CHAPTER 4

The Resistance

"The lads" of this study have adopted and developed to a fine degree in their school counterculture specific working-class themes: resistance; subversion of authority; informal penetration of the weaknesses and fallibilities of the formal; and an independent ability to create diversion and enjoyment.
—PAUL WILLIS (1977, 84)

As was the case with Willis's lads in the quote above, Indigenous children also produced countercultures in their resistance to the oppressive system that was Kamloops Indian Residential School. People rarely comply fully and easily to the introduction of oppression. Even with the controls already described well in place, students found time and space to express themselves and to produce a separate culture of their own within the school. Much of this culture was built on opposition to the severity of the rules and regulations guiding the students' daily lives. Another major facet of the resistance was expressed in the development of a subculture—one distinct from that being promoted by the religious orders. While it included challenges to the school officials, this culture also took on a life of its own. There were also students who sought refuge within the system as a means of immediate survival but whose actions led to eventual changes within it.

Stealing was common throughout the school. Because hunger was prevalent, food was the main target. It was stolen for immediate personal use, for sharing with smaller children, for barter, and to enhance the scanty meals of the dining room. Those who worked in the kitchen had easy access to food.

Because we're on that side [the girls' side], you're accessed to the food. [They] usually even take oranges in to their friends. If there is some whiny kid, then you can steal some oranges and go and give it to them. Then you got a piece of bread because it's all there.

You're the one that slices it, and Sister doesn't count how many pieces you got. (Josephine)

The sharing of stolen food led to the development of a particular subculture. As stealing became a complex operation, there were often several involved in the act itself, as well as guards on look-out and others involved in the distribution of the goods. Mildred's account demonstrates the complexity of the arrangements:

In my time, we were always hungry.... I seen them bringing in boxes and boxes of apples not too far from the dairy room. So I got these young women and I said, "How are we going to get some apples?" So for days and days the girls were scrounging around for strings, and my job was to look for spike nails.... We tied the strings together and there was an airhole in the root cellar. So we'd have all these girls watching out for us ... and we'd try to spike apples. That's how we used to get our apples to feed the little ones. We got caught and we got punished, but it took a long time because we supported each other in our crime.

The boys also found their way to the root cellar, sometimes with spears. Although they had access to the barns and all that was produced there, they sometimes resorted to eating cattle food or wild plants and berries in season.

> It depends on the time of year. In the fall ... there were berries and chokecherries and carrots and stuff like that, but as ... [they] went, we started eating grain, bran, or wheat. And they would mix this cow feed ... we used to eat that too, and we'd eat mangels, even.
>
> When we got higher up, we used to go down to the cellar and steal whenever we could.... Now, this time of year [May], you know those rose bushes, they have that berry on them ... we'd eat that berry. Earlier in the spring, when the shoots come out on the rose bush ... we used to eat that. It's sweet.
>
> We used to eat those things like wild onions, and you wouldn't believe it ... that mustard weed. That's awful. That was toward spring, when the cellar was empty. (Leo)

Food was uppermost in many students' minds. Several people mentioned gathering berries of all kinds and carrying them to eat as snacks. This action was not permitted by the supervisors, but as more than one person proudly claimed, "We never get caught." Mildred described how useful her bloomers had been.

> We used to go in the provision room downstairs, and there used to be buckets and buckets ... full of dried prunes, apricots, apples, raisins, nuts that they used to cook for the staff only. And boy, we didn't let them have it all.... We'd duck in there if it was open and grab a handful of this and a handful of that, shove it up your

bloomer legs. Fill it up and take off down the hall and go into the bathroom and take it all out.... We'd go around nibbling on that. And then other girls that couldn't steal would barter for it.

The fact that something of a routine developed around this stealing indicates that it was a frequent occurrence. Because of the limited amount of food supplied by the school, the children depended on their stealing and bartering. It became an integral and exciting part of daily life, one in which the children, unless they were caught, could feel some sense of power and control.

Another routine was established by a group of boys who worked in the dairy, using their position to institute a complicated process that ensured a more nutritious and tastier breakfast.

At night, one of those that separated the milk ... would come along and tap on that window from the outside.... He'd have a beer bottle full of cream. I'd take it and put it down in that space in the chaff and leave it till morning.... Then, after we clean the horses and feed them ... I put that cream in my boot.... And then, I'd take it in to breakfast and we'd put that on our mush.... I was the carrier. We done that and never got caught. (Leo)

At this point, sheer hunger was refined to a taste for cream. Important to note is the camaraderie created by common involvement in the crime. One can imagine the feelings of satisfaction the boys might have had as they feasted on their pilfered gains.

The search for power also had implications for students who served as agents of the supervisors. Some children would tell the authorities about their peers' misdemeanours. Because these informants had to be controlled, those who were misbehaving frequently built in methods for restraining them. At times students used the threat of informing as blackmail, as Julie described in the following example.

> We'd crawl along this ditch and get to the apple orchard and sneak apples back.... [Two boys] were stealing apples, and we hadn't got to the apple orchard yet. But they were on their way back, so we threatened if they didn't give us any apples, we were going to squeal on them. So they gave us some apples.

This incident took place in the late fifties, when an apple orchard was in production at the school. Shortly after, it was levelled to make room for a new dormitory building. The most amazing aspects of the stealing were its prevalence and the complexity of the various schemes for acquiring and distributing the goods.

The stealing of wine was also brought up as a recurring incident in the school. Minnie recalled,

> Gee, some kids, some boys and girls, they must have steal some wine. That's wine the priest used. They must have steal some, [but] they don't get drunk over wine.

Julie, who attended in the 1950s, reported the following scheme. She had been assigned to clean up the back of the chapel after the priest said Mass.

> Then this one day, this one boy knocked on the back door. So I opened the door to check what was there, and he looked at me and said, "Oh, where's C____?" and I said, "She doesn't work here anymore. I do." So that was that; he went away.

And about the third time, I was back there again and he knocks on the door and says, "I've got a nickel if you can fill this little jar up." So I says, "With what? Salt water? You got to be crazy." And he says, "No, no, not holy water. I want wine." And I got big eyes, "No way. Go away." So that lasted for about, I think, a week I held out.

And then we had a candy store every Sunday morning.... Everybody else was going to buy candy, and here I am with no money and wanting candy.... So that Sunday, the same guy came and knocked on the door. "Please fill this up," he said. "I'll give you a dime." So I said, "Okay." I took the jar and there was three gallons opened, so I took a little bit out of each one to fill the thing up, and he gave me the dime.

So away he went and ... I was really spooky—I mean I was scared. I went out and knelt down and prayed in front of that altar ... "I'll never, ever do this again. I promise." I swore up and down I wouldn't.... Then nothing seemed to happen to me. I checked myself out; my hair was still there. And I didn't have nits.... I never got sick or anything, so I thought that was pretty good.

So then·he come again.... I would sell to them, but I would take it out of each jar. And then if it looked like I might have taken too much, I would put a little water in the wine.... I never got caught at it neither. I quit praying. I did that for two years.

This delightful story indicates the degree to which an individual in the school might be involved in a form of "organized crime." The lessons the seller may have learned were significant ones: stealing was profitable, and one could stall the buyer to achieve a larger profit. Stealing wine that was used by the priest initially elicited prayer, but when immediate retribution failed to materialize, it became just business. Not only was the theft accomplished, she also learned to cover her tracks. Additionally, the boys who were paying for the wine were engaged in an interesting process. In both cases, the amount of wine was insignificant. Reportedly, it was divided among several boys. Again, within a repressive situation, the children could gain some sense of self-esteem in repeatedly succeeding at their self-assigned task. The students' awareness of the chinks in the armour of the oppressor provided hope for their survival and growth as individuals with agendas of their own.

Defiance manifested itself in ways other than thievery. Alternating between verbal and non-verbal defiance, Mildred dealt with the injustices of the system.

> That's why the name-calling, I used to call the nun [in Secwep-emctsín] … that's "dirty-behind nun."
> And the thing I remembered when she used to strap me…. I knew I was going to get five or ten straps on each hand, and I knew it was going to draw blood—but I would remind myself, "It's not going to hurt." Just so I can make you angry, I'm not going to let you know it hurts, and I would just stare at her in the face … and I wouldn't even let a drop, a tear come down. God, that used to make her mad. She'd even take me and shake my head and say, "The devil is in you so strong. How am I going to beat the devil out of you?" She'd put me in a dark place and tell me to stay there.
> I was a bad example for the rest.

With her dignity relatively intact and the nun's frustration leading her to make a display of outrage, Mildred felt she had won the battle. She was not humiliated because she did not cry. Although she was punished, she maintained her control. Other people spoke of maintaining their dignity through silence. Silence, often interpreted as passivity by Euro-Canadians—whose culture is more vocal—for the Indigenous is a sign of strength.

Anna showed her anger by silencing herself. In a later incident, she did so in a more dramatic way. Her mother, who had little money, had managed to send her two beautiful new blouses. She was told that she could keep only one and must give the other away.

> She [the nun] did not know or understand anything about home and how hard it was for my mum to get things, and I know this. And yet here is a system and so if she says so, that be done. Well, you just numb yourself.... You make a choice and you numb yourself to that hurt.

The fact that Anna saw herself making an active choice not to speak out about her hurt also gave her a sense of self-esteem. She realized that the nun did not know about her life, as she did. In that knowledge, she was stronger than the person causing her pain. She seemed to understand the futility of trying to explain to this foreigner why the blouses were so important.

In another incident, the repercussions for the nun's ignorance were immediate.

> Everybody was getting sick, and we all had to take castor oil. So God has ways to get even too.... At home I found out I could not take it.... Sister said, "You're no different than the rest of them." ... She made me take it. It came right back on her apron.... It was funny, and I pretended I was apologetic and I got cleaned up. (Anna)

Anna knew that she had tried to warn the nun. When her admonition was ignored, she inwardly rejoiced at the outcome. It gave her confidence to realize she was right: the nun's failure to respond brought its own retribution.

Incidents of this nature were viewed as great jokes on the supervisors. The "Indian dancing" episode mentioned previously is another example of this kind of resistance against the people in control. All the girls knew that Charlotte's dance was a mockery. Because of her fearless performance and the nun's acceptance of it as bona fide Indian dancing, she became an accepted group member with the other students, who found her behaviour hilarious.

For some students, language was another area for defiance. Again the betrayers had to be watched for, but some students served to educate newcomers about situations where Indigenous languages could be used without fear of reprisal.

> First year, I guess we were, and Leona came and we were all talking Shuswap.... She said to us, "You're never to get caught talking your language.... You'll get whipped, you'll really get punished." ... So we were careful after that not to be caught speaking.... When we were way out there, we'd talk together in our language. (Anna)

Archie, who attended in the fifties, recalled that he found it "tough for about a year. I was kind of careful where I used it." One Tsilhqut'in speaker, Maria, held defiantly to her language within herself because there were few others at KIRS who spoke it.

> I remembered trying to remember some words.... I was trying to remember one word, and that was "squirrel," and it was so easy....
> I remember struggling with it all day and trying to remember.

And then at night when I went to bed, I kept thinking about it, and I thought and thought and then it came up—"dltg."

Maria implicitly recognized the importance of maintaining contact with her roots through language. Even as she worked alone to remember, she felt a strong need to keep the words in her thinking vocabulary. The time for reunion with other Tsilhqut'in speakers was inevitable. For her, the language never lost its power and influence. She now teaches the language to those who want to learn.

Connecting with the opposite sex was another major preoccupation, particularly for some of the older students. The kitchen presented ideal opportunities for exchanging looks, quick words, and sometimes notes as the boys delivered milk, cream, and eggs. Lineups for meals and time in the chapel were other prime times for exchanges, including the oft-mentioned technique of mirror flashing.

They're not always just hovered over all the time. Like when I worked in the kitchen, those boys came for the garbage. You saw them in church every morning.... A lot of them, they had mirrors. So if you had a boyfriend in the back, you had a little mirror in front of your hymn book.... There were notes constantly flying back and forth somehow or another. There were communications. (Josephine)

For communicating with boys, another complex system was developed—again with care to avoid the tattlers—with deliveries made by messengers. One particularly ingenious method of note passing was devised by a girl who worked in the kitchen: she cut an extra-thick slice of bread, cut a space in the middle, and hid a note there, which was delivered to her boyfriend's table. Older teenagers sometimes managed to meet at the riverbank. Mildred commented,

> Nature is so strong. You can't help it; you can never destroy nature. Your body grows…. I don't care if you cover it up with layers and layers of clothes, it is still doing its thing as a human being.

The resistance to an unnatural control of normal human feelings was strong and effective. Despite the school's intensive efforts to completely segregate the sexes, communication occurred.

For the girls, curling hair and using makeup constituted another related form of resistance. These practices were probably perceived by the school staff as manifestations of the evil influence of white culture. For the children, they were another way of expressing a small amount of control within the authoritarian structure in which they found themselves.

> You were not allowed to put makeup on your face or let alone put a kiss curl in your hair…. If you tried, the nun would grab us by the top of the head and drag us under the sink and turn it on full blast…. Many's the time I got half-drownded. (Mildred)

Mildred also remembered Sunday afternoon walks with pleasure and a touch of defiance.

> We'd pool our bits of monies together and … [two girls would] buy a tube of lipstick and rouge and powder and cold cream…. On Sunday afternoon when we'd go for a long walk, we would make sure we were way up front where the nun is in the rear. And when we heard her blow the whistle … we used to carry a

little wet cloth with us. We'd wipe that stuff off and then we'd run
back.... I guess we must have looked like a bunch of clowns.

Each small step out of line was an important one in self-definition.
In a society determined by the powers of priests and nuns, the students' self-produced subculture was an important and fundamental
aspect of survival.

Even students who found cooperation with school authority
palatable under most circumstances became defiant in defence of
the injustices dealt to lawbreakers. Joe told of the following incident:

> I became a kind of an advocate for some of the people who I
> thought couldn't help themselves. I often became too outspoken
> in helping a person out of a jam. In trying to rationalize why
> they did it, why one was caught with carrots in his shirt, I had to
> explain he was hungry, somebody took his meat or his porridge
> away from him. So he was punished and, I suppose because I
> challenged the supervisor in front of the whole group, I was pun-
> ished with him.... After a while, I got my rewards for it ... he'd slip
> me a carrot for a retainer fee.

With this behaviour, a new role in the subculture was defined—that
of the advocate. Even the resistance movement itself had complexities; along with the advocacy role came a fee for services.

Eventually, the supervisor decided that this particular student,
Joe, could be enticed into supporting the system. He was put in
charge of a cleaning team. But when his team cleaned so quickly
and efficiently that he could lead them out to the playground for
recreation while the other teams were still working, the supervisor
did not approve.

It backfired on us. We'd finish in half the time, we'd go off, and
they'd call us back. They added another task to us ... instead of
rewarding us.... I said [to my gang], "We were betrayed ... we'll
just do ordinary work." (Joe)

The message to this instigator was clear. Playtime was not an appropriate occupation for boys who should be cleaning, and no rewards
were available for efficient work. One should use all the time prede-
termined by staff as necessary to complete the task. Although Joe
unwillingly cooperated, he saw the system for what it was: incapable
of dealing with and supporting efficiency of this nature.

Clique-like gangs were typical of life on the boys' side of the school.
The four males interviewed each made reference to the gangs. They
took a life of their own apart from the dictates of the school and over
the years operated with only occasional attempts at control by the
supervisors. Leo described the groups as follows:

They weren't that big of a group. The older boys, some of them
were dominating the rest of the kids, and they had the kids ter-
rorize the younger ones. That was going on all year. They couldn't
report it. If they ever reported it to the staff, they would be beat
up. They got away with it.

Other comments about the cliques suggested that school personnel
were either unaware of their existence or, more likely, they simply
ignored what they could not control. By the late fifties, the factions
had become more clearly defined and were on occasion extremely
competitive.

See, you had your clans. Every reserve was separate. I had cousins
in Bonaparte and Ashcroft, so Kamloops and Bonaparte, we really

stuck together. Then I was sort of the clique leader. I gradually had Chase brought in and then some of Lytton after that. Just about all of us [intermediate boys] were in: forty-two of us, to be exact.

It got pretty hot and heavy, the scrapping. There was one group trying to lead one way. and I was leading the other way.... The supervisors couldn't do nothing. (Sam)

Eventually the "scrapping" led to preparations for a major battle for leadership. When somebody "squealed," everybody was herded into the recreation room, where they were relieved of their weapons, including brass knuckles, clubs, and switchblades. The supervisor's comment was that this was police business, not school business. The fight did take place eventually, under less public circumstances. Sam's final comment on the situation was, "He was doing it just for show.... Them forty-two were my people."

The cliques were involved in less confrontational daily activities such as sending runners to town to buy alcohol during the Friday night movies, food theft, and other minor "crimes." Their success was based on students' need to feel a sense of belonging, experience the rush of adventure, and exercise choice and control in their lives. As the former leader wisely pointed out, "The point [for fighting] only come to the surface once a year. But what it really was, was below the surface in here [pointing to heart]" (Sam). Strong reactions to the authoritarian environment in which the boys lived exhibited itself at these times, but the boys felt the inhumanity of the system continually.

Joe, who chose not to become involved in the groups after his initial encounter with "the meanest group of people I ever met in my life," offered this analysis:

> I would imagine that if you're not feeling good about yourself, you
> begin to look for weaker ones ... and you get your licks in before
> time passes by.... Those who intended to make fun of us when we
> started probably were not feeling good about themselves—about
> their progress, their life. Being sad about leaving the comforts
> of home just like we were, [they] found us to be the weakest....
> Looking back, I thank them for it ... because it put some strength
> into us.

He chose to set himself apart and immerse himself in his academic
work. Because the nature of the groups changed over the years, gener-
alizations based on any particular time may be somewhat inaccurate.
Whether people banded together for mutual support and a sense of
family or it was the stronger establishing and demonstrating their
superiority probably varied over time. The gang of intermediate boys
described initially fell into the former category; they had originally
come together to repel the control of the seniors. As time went on and
their strength grew, the excitement of the organization perpetuated it.
Within the oppressive system, the gang provided a resistant force and
became oppressors in their own right. People who suffer oppression
frequently react by oppressing others. Because the children lived in an
inhumane environment, they learned to act in inhumane ways.

Josephine decided that rather than actively resist, she would
make herself an integral part of the school system in order to survive.
When she arrived at KIRS, she quickly realized that cooperation with
the nuns would lead her to a place of privilege and some power.

> Once I learned to respect the nuns ... when you done as you were
> told and worked hard, you got little promotions. You no longer
> have to work in the hallways or in the bathrooms. You don't have

to scrub anymore. You went up the ladder. You went up in where the nuns are, their quarters. You started to work there and then from there, you got to graduate to where the priests' quarters are and then into the chapel part, where it's cleaner and easier.

Then in the kitchen, too, it's up to you. If you want to remain in the scullery, if you think it's fine, then that's where you stayed, because you're not trying to advance and get into the staff cooking.... Cooking for [the staff] was more fun than cooking for the children.... You're accessed to all that beautiful food on the staff side. And if you so like, you can just fill up on there and never mind all that mushed-up food.

Josephine attributed her practical approach to her parents. Because she was the eldest sibling in a large family, she had always been expected to work very hard—perhaps harder than children with older siblings or those from smaller families. She knew discipline through necessity. Rather than actively resisting the system, she chose to work it to her advantage. In her privileged position, she gained considerable control over her life and, as a result, developed a sense of self-esteem.

Another form of active resistance was to run away. From the time the school began, children exercised this option. For some it was a thrill and a temporary break from school; for others it was a graphic plea to those at home to save them from their misery. Minnie, who attended early in the century, recalled,

Gee, one time six girls run away. It was at night; they put the sheets out the window.

They have to [go back]. Somebody look for them on the Indian reserve. They found them down ... Ben's home. They take them back.

They didn't stay too long, about one day and a half, maybe.... [They ran away] just for fun, maybe, fed up with going to school. They asked me to go. I told them, "No, I don't want to go, they'll just bring me back to the school." I didn't go.

Children who ran away were punished severely; the ones who were brought back had their heads shaved or their hair cut very short. Leo remembered,

They always came back. They got them back. I don't remember anybody getting away completely.... Some got expelled—they got twenty lashes and then they got expelled.... Father had a strap, it was about an inch, inch and a half, maybe. And there was two doubled and they were riveted together. He used that.

Josephine remembered a specific incident.

They'd been planning for weeks on end, packing stuff and hiding it outside. And then one night they all went to bed with their nightgown over their clothes.... A girlfriend and myself watched all this. How exciting. Anyways they went one by one down the fire escape.... There used to be a watchman.... You could see the light every time he came around the windows ... so probably these girls timed him.... I guess when they got around the corner then they all ran. You could hear them on the rocks.... Crazy us, we gave them an hour and then a friend of mine said, "I'm going to go and knock on Sister's door and tell her some of the girls are missing." It took quite a while; the last one took about a month before they found her.

Although these students all returned to the school, other runaways, particularly in later years, did not come back. It was not uncommon for children to run away and then be kept home by their parents.

Others who ran were not so lucky. In the school's official registers of 1947, the following note is the final entry for three boys: "Absconded Noon, Sept. 24. Killed in freight wreck Sept. 27" (Kamloops Indian Residential School 1947, n.p.). Another student who attended in the early sixties hitchhiked home after running away and was raped. Her parents sent her back to school, but when the resultant pregnancy became evident, she was expelled. Running away was one of the ways students showed their unhappiness. Before the options of day school on reserves and public school existed, stringent laws forced the return of most of the fugitives.

Parental and political involvement in the school, although infrequently sought or acted upon by administration, provided support for the children in their resistance to the injustices of the system. In 1913, Chief Louis of Kamloops expressed his dissatisfaction with the school during the proceedings of the now infamous McKenna-McBride Commission. Just as they aimed to cut off portions of reserve land, the commissioners, prime examples of Freire's cultural invaders (1970, 150), apparently came not to listen but—with their minds already made up—to persuade.

CHIEF LOUIS: I expected to see my people improve when they first went to Industrial School, but I have not seen anything of it. When they come out from school they don't seem to have improved much....

THE CHAIRMAN: Are you not getting the benefit of that to some extent? For instance can you write?

A. I write in my heart only.

Q. Can you write with a pen?

A. No.

Q. Don't you have to apply now and again to some of these children who have been to school to write for you?

A. Yes.

Q. And that is some help, is it not?

A. Yes.

Q. And some of them can read?

A. Yes, they bring me news.

Q. Well, the school is doing some good then?

A. Well, yes.

Q: I have seen the Indian children go through their examination, and have seen them pass their examinations quite as well as any white children I have ever seen, surely that is improving them, is it not?

A. Yes.

(British Columbia Royal Commission on Indian Affairs 1913, 15–76)

With that, the recorded interview ended. Rather than seeking to understand Chief Louis's concerns, the chairman silenced them by indicating that from the white perspective, improvement was taking place. Needless to say, there was no follow-up to the concerns expressed.

Leo recalled a number of the chiefs visiting the school in the thirties.

There wasn't very many that complained ... because we knew it wouldn't go out anyway. It was censored. But the odd note got out, and so they invited all the chiefs. I know about three times, four times while I was there.... Around 1937, '38, they invited all the chiefs from all surrounding areas that had children there.... Then they'd give us a decent meal while the chiefs were there. That's no good.

On these visits—usually held in response to chiefs' concerns about their children's complaints of hunger—school personnel made efforts to present the school in a good light. While it is normal to have good food when guests are invited, the quality served during these visits cast doubt on the children's accusations and may have calmed the parents' apprehensions. In 1946, after much lobbying, Chief Andrew Paull, president of the North American Indian Brotherhood, was permitted to address a parliamentary committee appointed to consider revisions to the Indian Act (Special Joint Committee 1947, 419). He presented First Nations people's apprehensions about a number of issues, including the residential school. Mildred recalled,

Parents were beginning to complain about the way the children were being fed and ... the way their children were being treated.... The Indian people themselves started fighting for integration. Then in 1945, we got together with the late Andy Paull ... and from then on we started fighting against residential schools.... They fought for better education, they fought for better treatment. They found out a lot of these young people ... didn't have no chance in life unless they were [from] a strong family or you were a strong person.... You had to be told what time to eat, what time to go to bed, what time to bathe, what time to change, all this type of thing.

Through political action, stimulated by their own and by their children's experiences at the school, parents began the twenty-year campaign to close the school.

On another occasion, strong action on the part of the parents had immediate effect. The children were upset by the cruel treatment they were receiving at the hands of the music instructor.

We had been sneaking letters home to our parents [about] how we were being treated here.... The Chief from home came one weekend with two other chiefs. They came and ... we went to the parlour and visited with him. He told us what they were planning to do, said, "If anybody gets beat up again by this Mr. _____, we want to know about it."

So this one night we were all down in the dining room and we were practising hymns. And girls were getting irritated because he said he wasn't satisfied.... And this was getting towards midnight, and we were getting tired. He went along to the senior bench and he listened. He put his ear right down to their mouth, and A_____ wasn't even singing. She was mad. There was another girl.... He slapped A_____ but [the other girl] ... answered him back, and that just blew him. He hit her with the harmonica and she started bleeding. It split her head. And that's when everybody started screaming, and they all ran out when they seen blood. And he just went wild, grabbed her and shook the hell out of her.

And she ran.... Within two days, [the chiefs] were here.... And I remember ... [one] attacking the guy. He told him if he didn't leave the school that he would charge him.... And I remember that old guy leaving.

The next year he came back in a brother suit; he became a brother.... And ... [the chief] came again when we told him that this Mr. _____ is a brother ... and he is back. And the chief came and really raised hell with him, told him "I don't care if you come camouflaged in a priest suit.... We told you to leave. We don't want you back. Get!" He disappeared, and we've never seen him since. (Mildred)

Although local politicians and parents had little power to affect the everyday life of the school, in extreme incidents such as the one described, they took power and wielded it forcefully. This moral support helped the children deal with the hardships of everyday life and inspired them to continue to believe in their people's strength.

Parents also became directly involved in their children's welfare. One person described her parents' horror at the head shaving and kerosene treatment for lice that her sister had received. The kerosene had burned the girl's head. While the children and parents were commiserating in the parlour during a family visit, the hapless priest walked in. "Dad just grabbed him and shook him up." (Julie) The irate father tried to relieve his sense of helpless frustration caused by his daughter's plight. Julie described another visit by her parents. She was on a special diet to prevent allergies.

They tried to make me eat what everybody else was eating.... I wouldn't eat, so she made that plate sit there until the next meal, and I still wouldn't eat.... This went on for four meals.... We snuck a letter out.... So the next day, my mum and dad both came.... They knew we were eating, so they just walked right down to that

room.... My dad walked into where the nuns and priests were
eating ... and he said to that priest, "And you expect my daughter
to eat this slop and you guys are in there eating like kings and
queens."

Following the ensuing altercation, all agreed that the special diet
would be reinstated. Julie and her parents created a small moment
of justice in a predominantly inhumane environment.

These pockets of resistance were significant at the Kamloops
Indian Residential School. Few students were not directly involved
in opposing the rules and regulations. At times, the oppression
produced countercultures—groups of children who defined roles,
projects, and ways of daily life for and with one another. They did so
by taking back some power without the sanction or, in some cases,
even the knowledge of those who officially held the power of administration. Although other aspects of the school also influenced the
children's development, these opposition movements live clearly in
people's memories as times of strength and resistance. Fascination
and fear were also recurring themes in their discussions of the
subcultures. There was wonder at the inventiveness of children and
the complexities of the roles which developed; there was fear for
the recklessness involved and the extent to which they went to
define their versions of power and control. At the same time, not
one interviewee involved in thievery, gang warfare, or any other
form of resistance indicated any sense of regret for their actions. In
retrospect, they saw them as the actions of strong people against a
system that too often worked to degrade and dehumanize them.

CHAPTER 5

Going Home

Who are you, who are you? I have to admit to them, to myself
I am an Indian.

—FRANCES KATASSE (IN GOODERHAM 1969, XI)

Eventually the time came to leave school. Some students were sent
home when they became ill. Others who ran away were allowed
to stay home. Some students, those who died at the school, never
went home.

> She was a really good friend. Tattooing your hands [was common].
> And she done that, she used a common pin or needle … and wrote
> her initials on her hand and then it got blood poisoning from the
> ink. Like her hand was swelling and swelling. Two or three days
> later … she started getting a fever.
>
> So she showed the nun and they just sent her to bed. And
> when she must have been in bed about two days…. She was get-
> ting so she wasn't even herself…. And she just lay in bed, and two
> days later, she died. (Julie)

Other reports of death by those interviewed include an accidental
death by hanging when some children left a playmate who was pre-
tending to be an outlaw. The box he was standing on slipped out

from under him when no one else was there. By the time someone noticed he was missing from school, it was too late. Children who became ill with scarlet fever, tuberculosis, and other diseases were sometimes sent home or to hospitals. Many never returned to school.

Others left school when they reached the final grade offered, which for many years was grade 8. From 1951 to 1959, when high school was more widely instituted, a few students were given the opportunity to write provincial examinations, and they graduated. Beginning in 1960, high school students attended St. Ann's Academy in Kamloops (Secwepemc Cultural Education Society 1977, 4, 10).

Most of those interviewed credit the school with making them tough. In answer to the question, "What did you learn in school?" Sam replied, "To watch yourself and independence." Needless to say, academic subjects were much less important to him. Mildred summed up her experience in this way:

> All in all, my life hasn't really been that bad. It is just knowing I went through that humiliation and that hurt, that low self-esteem and having come out of it. And never letting that hate leave a scar on me. I don't hate anymore.... I do get angry, but it doesn't mean I hate anybody.... That's the strength I got from what I went through. In a lot of ways I have this place [KIRS] and the people that put me through it to thank for the strength I got ... a lot of strength to fight back, and that strength I got is what's made me into the woman I am today.

Joe concurred.

> In retrospect, there are times when I thank [the tough boys] for it because they put fight into me physically and mentally. They

helped make me mentally tough because I met other tough situations which were not as tough as that.... And having survived that, I think I can survive anything.

For other students, the school's stern discipline was at least temporarily effective. As Maria said, "My experience in residential school made me a passive, obedient person." She felt strongly the oppressive nature of the onslaught against her culture.

I would sum it up by saying that they were definitely stripping us of our culture.... There might have been workers who didn't know exactly what was happenin' but they had to follow rules. There was no doubt that they were driving out the culture.

Some of the lessons had opposite effects to those intended.

They stress religion over everything else.... Going to church was more important to them than the classes.... The religion part was habit.... It was just a thing you done day in and day out. If those kids would suddenly have to go and pray on the side of a mountain by themselves, they wouldn't know how.... I think when they were saying their grace for their meal, they were looking at what kind of ugly stuff they were getting.... Mass was celebrated in Latin, and we didn't know what we were saying.... It's just like a punishment, going to church. (Leo)

Leo commented also that he'd learned more about life while in the army than while he was at school. "In the school, we didn't learn anything about life other than read, and write, and arithmetic, and a low grade, and going to church."

When people finished school and returned home, some readjusted quickly to their family's ways. Sophie, always a keen learner, found going home exciting.

> I went home and I stayed home with my mother. I helped ... gathering foods and learning how to dry salmon ... experiencing the type of food and the [time of] year that they ate. I had to acquire the taste to it because I had forgotten it after so many years.... I found that I'm easy to adjust to things, and I'm always aware this was an experience I wanted to learn. I wanted to know, how did my parents survive here in the winter?

For a few, the idea of succeeding in the larger society was combined with the idea of being Secwépemc. Joe, who was hesitant about his plans after graduation, received strong words of advice from an Elder.

> I complained, "I would like to be a doctor or a teacher. but I'm just an Indian, and Indians don't become doctors." And I'd keep on this. "I would like to go to big school—university, they call it.... There's nobody there who's Indian."
>
> She was a little tiny woman. She jumped up and stamped her feet.... She said, "That's an excuse.... You have hands, you have a mind, you have people who lived long before you who had a control of life.... That is Indian. That is Shuswap. You have it flowing through your veins.... It is because you are an Indian that you do well, whatever you do."

This advice was instrumental in giving Joe the strength to accept his Indigeneity with pride and to build a successful and happy life upon that foundation.

For others, cultural clashes surfaced. For the women who left school in the forties, arranged marriages were the focus of conflict. Josephine, who returned to work at the school in order to avoid her parents' decision, enlisted her brother's support. He said,

> "Write to Father. We'll write him a letter and we'll tell him all about it. You don't want to get married, and you want to keep on going to school...." So both of us ... wrote a long letter ... and quite a few days later, my mum and dad got a letter that I was to return to school. And my mum was very angry.

Sophie eventually married the person her mother had chosen. However, she did so when she felt ready and only after spending considerable time working.

> Still I was yearning for more learning. After one year at home ... I guess the reason I wanted to get out of there was my mother wouldn't leave me rest: I had to get married. But I didn't want to; I wasn't ready yet.... I wanted to know what it was to be independent. And I fought my mother; I rebelled against her.

Sophie worked for different families in the area as a housekeeper and began learning in earnest.

> The one thing I stole from the school ... was an old torn-up dictionary....
>
> The thing that I learned when I was with [the people I worked for], we used to sit around the breakfast table and dinner table, and I used to pay attention to their conversation. I'd hear a word. One word that always sticks in my mind ... was the word "naive." I thought, "Gee, that's a new word." After I finished eating, I

excused myself, I ran up to my bedroom. I looked through my dictionary and I studied how you spell it and how you pronounce it and what is the meaning. Then a few days later, I'd try to use it in my own conversation.

And there were many words after that.... I read books one after another ... and I began to learn. I learned how to express myself and I learned how to talk a little better than I learned in [KIRS].

Although the reading skills she had learned in school allowed Sophie to proceed in this way, unfortunately the school had never provided an opportunity for her desire for an investigative and stimulating education driven by curiosity. Significant learning began only after she left the oppressive system and found a new sense of purpose and self-worth.

For both Josephine and Sophie, the decision to defy their parents' wishes for immediate marriage was in all likelihood based on their experiences at school. Whether it was a part of the school's tactics to attack the idea of arranged marriages or school had merely taught them defiance is an interesting question. Nevertheless, both women did defy their parents' wishes. Neither mentioned any influence from the school regarding arranged marriages. However, because Europeans had discontinued the practice, one may assume that school personnel would have opposed the idea and consequently supported the women in their opposition to the tradition.

The area of sexuality provided another focus for clashes. Whereas children had been taught in school to de-emphasize sexuality, in traditional Secwépemc culture, it was seen as a natural part of life.

Mildred, who attended school for only three years, described her grandmother's teachings about sex.

> When I was growing up and getting into womanhood, [Granny] told me ... "You got a beautiful body, you look after that body.... Don't abuse it." She told me about the facts of life, she told me how to cleanse my body.... I'd look at myself and I'd say to myself, ... "Granny always says my body is beautiful. Look after it with great respect."

In direct contrast to this acceptance of the physical self, the religious people at school had insisted on covering the body at all times. Women reported that they had been told to wear their underwear while in the shower and that their breasts were never to be seen, not even while they changed clothes. Sex was not a topic of discussion in the school.

> The nuns were really pathetic.... Later on, as an adult, I talked to them. They said, "We thought you kids knew lots," because we came from the reserve. And we knew nothing. (Anna)

Charlotte, who attended school eight years later, found that what she learned about sex in school had tremendous repercussions in her life.

> I was really scared.... Every time I went to the washroom ... it's wrong. You better not touch yourself.... If I looked at somebody: ... lust, sex, and I got scared of those sexual feelings. And I didn't know how to handle them.... What really confused me was if intercourse was a sin, why are people born? ... It took me a really long time to get over the fact that ... I've sinned: I had a child.

Although both traditional Secwépemc and Catholic religions emphasized that sex should be confined to marriage, the methods for
presenting these views are contrasting. Traditional Secwépemc
values emphasize the positive, that the body is beautiful and should
be cared for accordingly.

> I've always been a Shuswap and I've always been a woman. I
> looked after myself, and I always believe that where my children
> come from, that's like a temple. (Anna)

The Catholic controls described by interviewees stressed the
negative: sex was closely tied with sin, and daily contact with the
opposite sex could lead to sin in thought, word, or deed. Consistent
with the tyrannically punitive controls imposed by the school personnel, the threats of sin and hellfire were visualized as appropriate
means of minimizing sexual thoughts of any kind. Other than these
threats, the most common control was to ignore the existence of
sexuality—to cover the body and to never mention the topic. This
negativism clashed with Secwépemc ideas and, for a number of
the people interviewed, created problems which required careful
resolution in later life.

Indigenous languages were another significant issue for people going home. As has been noted, the use of Secwepemctsín,
Nlaka'pamuxtsn, Tsilhqut'in, or any other Indigenous language was
forbidden in the school. Although second generations attending the
residential school frequently did not speak their language, the first
generation managed to maintain their knowledge, at least partially.
Many who started school at nine or ten either retained their fluency
or regained it with the recent developing awareness of the centrality

of language to world view. Those who left school in the earlier years found some need to readjust to using the language. Leo commented,

> You know something funny about speaking your own language? When I first come out of school, I was embarrassed to speak my language in front of white people.... Now I speak Shuswap anyplace and anytime ... but it took about three or four years ... to get away from that embarrassment of speaking it on the street.... They just about brainwashed us out of it.

Within these words lies a clear indication of the school's intent to eradicate Indigenous languages. Not only were students forbidden to speak them in school, they were also convinced that their use of Indigenous languages was an indication of persisting inferiority. The import attached to public humiliation for Secwépemc people has already been discussed. In this case, it was included in the indoctrination which, it was hoped, would serve as a control even after students had left the direct influence of the perpetrators.

That some people did not manage to resist these controls is indisputable. Although one person who continues to speak his language puzzled about those who swore that they had forgotten how to speak their languages, Julie shed some interesting light on the subject.

> I spoke Indian when I went to school. I could speak some English because [my sisters] went to school. So you learned. They told you when they came back, ... "You can't speak Indian; you got to speak English. If you speak Indian, you get whipped." It took them a long time to get it out of me. And to this day ... I speak some words ... but I don't speak it fluently. I used to be able to speak it fluently before I went to school.

She then described attendance at a spiritual sweat ceremony years after attending KIRS at which she could temporarily speak her language fluently. The possibility exists that psychological controls arising from the school's disapproval led her to repress her knowledge of the language, preventing her from speaking it. If this is the case, then the possibility also exists that some key therapy, perhaps, to create understanding of the system which attempted to "get it out of" her might enable her to speak the language again. Discussion with Joe, who has returned to his language after time away, confirms this possibility.

> Most of my Shuswap was learned from birth to the time I come to school.... And I left the language until ten years ago. That's roughly a period of thirty years when I didn't have the language spoken. I spoke intermittently with some Elders, but when I returned to the language, I had no difficulty at all. I'm fluent. I was fluent when I was eight, and I teach the language now.

Anna, who commented, "I shouldn't even say I'm proud. I had to put words to it. It's my language; it's who I am," provided more insight into the notion that a language learned in childhood remains buried in the mind.

> There are a lot of words I haven't said yet, but it's in my computer [brain]. I found that out last year. I never said "SI' gh gee" and yet I know it. I never said it through my mouth.... There's a lot of words in there I haven't said through my mouth yet, because those were put in when I didn't need to use those words. Now, as an adult, I need to use them.

For those who came to school with their language, their chances of retention were relatively good, particularly with summer visits to reinforce its use. The school's biggest effect on language use could perhaps be called secondary. Although punishing children for speaking their language did not eradicate it, many former students as adults consciously chose not to teach their children an Indigenous language as a way to save them from the punishments incurred for its use at school. Others believed the propaganda designed to convince them that Secwepemctsín was unimportant. This generational control has had devastating effects on the children whose parents attended residential school. Many of them have never learned their Indigenous language.

For many former students of KIRS, the religious teachings have led to confusion and lack of faith.

> There was a lot of times I used to wonder why God didn't answer my prayers. People said if you pray, God will hear you. It seemed like I prayed so much—I used to pray to go home and ... you just couldn't go home. I used to wonder what kind of God it was.... It was hard to take religion. (Beverly)

Beverly has since moved away from the Catholic Church, which had little meaning for her. Others, like Anna, have managed to combine their Catholic beliefs with traditional ones.

> I'm a Catholic today, a practising Catholic. And whatever I believe from my ancestry is real, and I believe in that. I want to live as best I could.... On my own spiritualism of my people, I know there was something there, and I know it's real.

> They [Catholic and traditional religions] are not [mutually exclusive], especially if you get away from the mortal sin and God's going to punish you.... God is love. He made each of us.

This positive attitude to adapting the two approaches to spirituality has led Anna to a peaceful resolution of conflict between the two.

Not all people who attended KIRS managed to reach such a compromise when it came to family life. Former students who are now parents recognize the deficiencies in their experience with family units. Beverly commented, "The residential schools took away the responsibility of the parents, because the parents didn't see the kids all year." Children learn parenting skills from the way they are parented. Those who spent eight, ten, or more years at KIRS had limited experience as family members. In the same way that their language use was based on the knowledge they gained before going to school, so their parenting skills could only draw on that limited experience.

Alcohol also became a force in the lives of some families. Some parents, heartbroken at the loss of their children and objects of continuing oppression from all aspects of the dominant society, escaped these pressures with alcohol. For some children, alcohol consumption became the norm on visits home.

> When we started coming home at Christmastime ... it was one big party. Even us kids got involved with the drinking. We sat there and got as drunk as everybody else did.... When I think about it, we really ... blame[d] Mum a lot for what happened. And I think that's probably another reason why she started drinking, was she thought we didn't need her anymore. (Julie)

Julie saw two forces related to school contributing to her mother's alcoholism. Her mother felt unneeded and, in all likelihood, felt that the children blamed her for sending them to school. On the one hand were the children pleading to stay home, and on the other were the government and the church insisting that she send them to school. A desire to escape from these inescapable pressures is understandable.

Suicide, the ultimate escape from a harsh reality, was another route taken by despairing people. Although none of the people interviewed mentioned victims of suicide, Beverly said that she contemplated it when her life appeared to be without meaning.

> I started to think, "Well, twelve years here. I don't want to be here for twelve years." By the time I was in grade 5, they used to let us go for walks.... I decided ... to go down to the Thompson River.... [It] was really high; it was springtime, I guess, and you could see that the water was deep, and I don't know how many times ... I used to think of drowning myself. I would be standing there and I would think, "Gee, life can't continue like this."

While blame for Indigenous suicides cannot be laid entirely on the residential school, the school certainly can be seen as a contributing factor to people's confusion over the values and meaning of life, as well as symptomatic of the social oppression that may lead to such attempts. Sexual and physical abuse were other sorrowful factors that caused students feel they simply could not take it anymore.

Perhaps one of the reasons for the strength of the people interviewed lies with the fact that the words and ways of the Elders and of their families still have tremendous influence in their lives and in the lives of many Secwépemc people. Despite years of residential schooling, parental and cultural values remained strong within the students' psyches.

> [Granny] had dreams. Before, I guess through my Catholic teach-
> ing, I thought dreams and all these other things were wrong, like
> sin. But in praying about it in my adult life ... we all have those
> powers. I've come to believe that. (Anna)

Traditional ways are integral to the lives of most of those interviewed. Anna also commented, "All the people from our way teach us, never use food in an argument.... You don't withhold food or abuse it in an argument. Food is sustenance."

Charlotte feels her grandmother's presence in her house, which she inherited.

> Her spirit is really strong in the house. Sometimes if I neglect to
> do something, she lets me know, or sometimes if I get balky ...
> she's got enough patience. She'll wait until I'm ready, because I
> sometimes get scared of what she is trying to teach me.

Charlotte described burning sage in her house as a cleansing method, which she learned by watching her grandmother. "I just watched her. She never told me nothing. She'd just get it and burn it." Anna describes a custom her grandmother practised with her that she now does with her own grandchildren.

> I remember her doing that to me, [gesturing] and saying, "Whsst,
> whsst." That was like every evening. And other times she would
> pat my hair.... I think she talked to me those times, but she used
> to always do that, "Whsst, whsst." I always find that funny. I do

that to my grandchildren. I wonder what that was all about, but my kyé7e used to do that to me.

Even in apparently insignificant little details, this unquestioning acceptance of the way people do things forms some of the basis for cultural identity, persistence, and strength. While another grandmother was being interviewed, her grandchildren—young adults—sat at a nearby kitchen table, preparing pine needles for "Granny's medicine." In so many ways, the traditions are perpetuated.

In the final analysis, the people interviewed for this book are survivors. Statistics of alcoholism and suicide speak to the suffering and pain of many who attended the school and, conversely, to the strength of those survivors. The participants—who were subjected to a massive onslaught against their culture and all it stood for—have, in a demonstration of the strength of the human spirit, grown, changed, developed, and at the same time, remained conscious of their ancestry.

Throughout the years, the survivors have resisted the cultural invasion around them. The people who attended KIRS were indubitably changed by their experience. However, neither government policy nor missionary fervour to assimilate Indigenous peoples was successful. Through pain, hunger, cold, sickness, and corporal punishment, the interviewees managed to remain their ancestors' children and to glean understanding of the importance of being Indigenous as an irrepressible part of their lives.

Summer scene at KIRS, ca. 1960. | *Kamloops Museum and Archives, 6274*

CHAPTER 6

KIRS 1987

The government asks Indians, "What do you want?" But they
don't understand we're different cultures and have different
answers to the question.
—MARINA TOM, *WISDOM OF THE ELDERS* (KIRK 1986)

The most outstanding feature that emerges from these stories of
Indigenous people attending the Kamloops Indian Residential
School is the extent and complexity of their resistance. The students,
in their wisdom, recognized the injustices of the system that attempted
to control them and transform them. In innumerable ways, they
fought for some control in an impersonalized system—for decent
daily lives without cold and hunger, and for the means to survive the
oppression around them while maintaining a sense of self and family. This strength has led to today's work in education by Indigenous
people throughout British Columbia and the world.

In 1985 and '86, when the original study for this book was conducted, the buildings that housed KIRS for so many years stood as
a historical reminder of the structure of Indigenous schooling since
the Europeans first arrived. However, unlike many other residential
school buildings, which have been abandoned, have fallen into dis-
repair, or have even been burned, many of the KIRS buildings were
then and still are a hive of activity, a tribute to the survival of the

Secwépemc people, a microcosm of the world of Indigenous control and Indigenous education today. All of the buildings were turned over to the Tk'emlúps te Secwépemc in 1978; since then they have been of increasing importance both culturally and economically. Major reorganization and development of the buildings continue. It's ironic that many of the buildings, which for so long were the centre of a cultural onslaught, are now the centre of Secwépemc governance, including cultural reclamation, advancement, and economic development. A tour of existing buildings as they functioned in 1987 reveals a fascinating collection of political and educational enterprises.

The senior girls' dormitory on the top floor of the east wing had become the field centre for the Native Indian Teacher Education Program (NITEP), a University of British Columbia program for prospective elementary teachers. Directly below was the college preparation program, organized by the Secwepemc Cultural Education Society and, even then, threatened by funding cutbacks by the Department of Indian Affairs. A Native Adult Basic Education Program was offered. On the main floor, a band-operated child care centre, Little Fawn Nursery, was thriving. It catered to Indigenous people who worked and studied in the various buildings and to people from Kamloops, who drove their children across the river. A qualified member of the Secwépemc Nation ran the centre; several other Secwépemc Nation members were employed in it. After-school care was available for children attending the band-run school next door. In the basement, a Montessori school run and predominantly attended by non-Indigenous people rented facilities from the band.

To the west was an efficient cafeteria. Most of the women who came to cook and organize the facilities had been students at the residential school. Much of the kitchen equipment from their school days was still in use. What memories must have circulated there? Now the kitchen was used to prepare meals for Elders' gatherings; for a variety of conferences, such as the one held in 1986 to discuss British Columbia's Master Tuition Agreement, a contentious bilateral agreement between federal and provincial governments; and for thrice-weekly meals for students and workers in the complex. The meals served in the infamous dining room differed greatly from those that had been served to residential school children. They regularly included bannock and salmon, and at least once, a sampling of steamed lichen. Across from the large dining room, which also served as a meeting hall for graduation celebrations and school Christmas concerts, was the smaller "priests' dining room." It offered a continuous supply of coffee for the maintenance staff and was used for lunches when fewer people were about during business holidays.

Up the central stairs from the cafeteria were a variety of offices used by groups like the now-disbanded Central Interior Tribal Council (CITC). This group separated over time as local control became an issue of increasing importance and the centralized focus of the group became somewhat inefficient. The now-deserted chapel was also located on this floor. Although it was still used occasionally for weddings and funerals, most of the Catholic ceremonies had moved to the restored heritage church in the central village of the reserve. A salmon enhancement project; the Western Indian Agriculture Corporation; and an underfunded but well-stocked resources centre (a vestige of the CITC) occupied the remainder of the floor. At the top of the central stairs was the Shuswap Nation

Tribal Council, a very active political organization of the Secwépemc bands of the area.

At the west end of the building, one could climb a flight of stairs to the Secwepemc Cultural Education Society. This extremely active group had many responsibilities. The director of the museum and archives had initiated the return of Secwépemc materials from other museums; now they were safely lodged in the current museum and heritage park.[6] Various personnel conducted primary research for educational and political purposes. A curriculum committee was finalizing two supplementary texts focused on Secwépemc experiences for elementary schools. A desktop publishing company was in development. A media centre had produced a number of videos in conjunction with the society's activities. A series of workshops focusing on skills from researching techniques to writing and publishing had been held. Secwepemctsín teachers participated in a number of professional development days there. Above the cultural centre, the empty senior boys' dorm awaited a new idea or project.

To the south of the large brick main building lay the "new" dormitory. Somewhat ironically, at that time it was being rented by the Kamloops Christian School for their classes. This independent school did attract a few Indigenous students whose parents felt that religious training was important and chose to remove their children from the public schools to attend. While some classes followed the BC curriculum, the older students used the ACE program, an American Christian correspondence program that focused on so-called Christian values.

---

6 Read about the museum and heritage park at https://tkemlups.ca/profile/history/our-language.

The new school dormitory building, ca. 1970. | *Kamloops Museum and Archives, R.B.A. Cragg fonds, #1989.009.056, #7 December 20, 1970, slide 3625*

Kamloops Indian School Residence, 1977: games in front of the school. | *Kamloops Museum and Archives, Sentinel fonds (unprocessed), File: June 1977, Envelope: MR808 June 16/77, Negative: #30A-31*

To the west of the main building lay the classroom block of the residential school, now torn down and replaced with a modern school building housing the Sk'elep School of Excellence for grades K–7.[7] In the eighties, it housed the Little Fawn Nursery and the three classrooms of what was then called the Seklep Elementary School. The former was administered and staffed by the Nation. In Kamloops in 1981, the band decided to move into control of their school in a gradual way. In cooperation with the local school district, the band opened Sek'lep School. Hiring Secwépemc teachers was the priority, and in most years, at least two of the three teachers were Secwépemc. In addition, a Secwepemctsín teacher and teacher's aide worked in the school. The teachers focused on the provincial curriculum, but emphasized Secwépemc content wherever possible. The school quickly grew from its initial single classroom and three grades to three classrooms with all elementary grades. Today, in 2022, it is one of the largest First Nations schools in British Columbia.[8]

Even in 1983, parents of five- to seven-year-olds generally felt very positive about the school when interviewed, primarily because their children were happy there. Many of the children had attended daycare or nursery school in the same building and, because it was next door to the band office, all were familiar with their surroundings. Comments such as, "He really likes school now," and "She never wants to miss a day," were most common. One parent, who had sent her child to the school on a trial basis for kindergarten, was particularly happy with her child's progress in the Secwepemctsín program. Another parent had watched her child change from a stubborn and

7 See https://skelep.com/.
8 Learn more at https://tkemlups.ca/departments/education/skelep-school-excellence/.

uncooperative child in public kindergarten to a happy grade 1 student at Sek'lep. In Kamloops, he had been teased about the length of his hair and had experienced the negativity of anti-Indigenous racism. In the Nation's school, however, he was taught to be proud of his heritage. His mother commented of the Secwépemc classroom teacher, "She knows what it's like to be Indian." The conflict of values that she had felt strongly when her son was in kindergarten had ceased to exist. Issues of political importance to Indigenous people were discussed in the school. One child reported that, on one occasion, when students had exchanged insults with some non-Indigenous children at the nearby religious school, the Secwépemc children reminded the others that they were on Indigenous land.

The list of activities and accomplishments in Indigenous education since the closure of the residential schools and the subsequent lack of success of many students in integrating into the public schools continues. It is tempting to say, as the Department of Indian Affairs is wont to do, that the future holds nothing but success. But the changes must be examined critically. None have been accomplished easily; all have been the subject of endless analysis and ongoing reform. While gaining control of some funding for education is in itself a major step, it cannot compare to the work that must follow. Taking over an entire education system is a long-term process. For Indigenous people, many of whom have had some of the worst schooling experiences imaginable, the task is even more formidable.

The residential schools themselves are closed. But their impact lives on. The experiences documented in this book continue to affect the lives of the people who lived them. Throughout the province and the country, thousands of First Nations people carry such stories in their hearts and minds. These are the stories that attest to the strength and perseverance of Indigenous cultures in Canada. These are the stories that must be told to all our children and grand-children so that they too can come to recognize and appreciate the history of the people who came before them and the power of their legacy of survival.

CHAPTER 7

Tsqelmucwílc:
We Return to Being Human

INTRODUCTION

When Randy Fred insisted that we revisit *Resistance and Renewal*, the first iteration of this book, I was very hesitant. When he persisted, I felt growing excitement about the possibilities of such a revisiting. This could be a time to fully recognize the people who had given me so much in telling me their stories of residential school so long ago. Furthermore, they would have an opportunity to add to their stories as they themselves circled back to thoughts of the Kamloops Indian Residential School and what it means to them now, in 2022.

As noted earlier, some people I approached were keen to be involved. What follows are their words as they share with readers how the years have affected them and their views of the school. In some cases, their children or grandchildren have written me; others have spoken directly to their own experiences.

I have ordered the contributions from the oldest of the former students interviewed to the youngest, and each former student has provided a description of themselves in their own words. The one exception to this order is the group of three who spoke to the Prime Minster of Canada when he finally visited Tk'emlúps te

Secwémpemc following the recovery of the 215 and have generously allowed me to reproduce their remarks here.

Minnie Dick with her husband, Sandy Adrian, September 1977, at Neskonlith. | *From the private collection of Jacqueline Jones. Photographer unknown*

Minnie Dick (1900–1987)
attended KIRS 1907–1908

REMARKS BY JACKIE JONES, GRANDDAUGHTER OF MINNIE DICK

The following is my compilation of some of the memories and thoughts of the late Minnie Dick's family—Judy, Jennifer, Janice, Beverley, Miranda, Shelley, and me.

How does one put in writing how important kyé7e Minnie was to us as we were growing up? All of us stayed with her for various periods of time, from when we were children to when we became adults. When we lived apart from her, we were never far from her. It is from these times that we learned to value Secwepemctsín and all the ways of the Secwépemc, including looking after oneself, looking after each other, looking after the land, and knowing that we are all related.

Minnie was born on August 4, 1900, in Secwepemculecw to Denys and Josephine Soule. She lived with her parents and brother, Alex Cwellyeta Dennis, at Ciyala. Minnie's father, Denys, had several siblings, so she and Alex were members of a large extended family. Minnie's early years were spent at Ciyala, where she learned gardening, root digging, fishing, buckskin work, and berry picking from her kyé7e Josephine and other relatives.

The family lived in an old comfortable log house next to their big apple orchard. The house sat near a creek at the base of the mountain overlooking the river and valley. At about age seven, Minnie was taken away from this beautiful home and family to attend what was then known as the Kamloops Industrial School. One can only imagine what was going on in her heart and her mind about why she had to leave Ciyala.

Fortunately, she did not stay at the school very long, because she had to return home to help care for a sick family member. When the 215 graves were discovered at the former residential school, our family pondered many what-ifs. What if she had stayed at the school and never went home, like the other 215 students? Would our spirits exist in other people? Would our spirits even exist? What if she had returned to the school and been abused and shamed for speaking Secwepemctsín? What if today we knew and spoke the Secwepemctsín that the Nation lost in their deaths? Because Minnie didn't stay long at the school, she was able to maintain and foster the ways of the Secwépemc and pass them on to her daughter and grandchildren. It was serendipitous that we received a residential school class picture with her in it at the same time the 215 grave sites were recovered. It seemed that she was asking us from the picture to remember her and all that she taught us about looking after ourselves, looking after one another, looking after the land, and not forgetting our people.

Eventually, she married Mike Joe Dick from Celewt and worked hard alongside him and his family tending to the garden, the fruit trees, the hayfields, and the horses. Their hard work was rewarded by the house dances that the Dick family and their neighbours had. On August 9, 1921, they were gifted with the birth of their only daughter, our mother, Rita. Rita herself attended Kamloops Indian Residential School for eight years, a time away from home and family that had a lasting impact on her life. Only her eldest daughter attended the residential school for a time. Eventually our mother took her out of the school and sent us all to public school. She said that the residential school was not a good place. Apart from this comment, she did not talk to us about the school or her experiences there.

After Mike died, Minnie lived with her second husband, Sandy Adrian. Together they gardened, picked berries, dug roots, harvested fruit, and speared and dried salmon in preparation for the winter. For spending money, they harvested vegetables at a farm in town and picked cones for the forestry service. She did all of this to help our mother raise her children. Minnie often looked after her great-grandchildren. Throughout the rest of their lives, our grandmother and our mother were never far apart and often lived together. I think it would be safe to say that Minnie lived for her daughter and her grandchildren. Living with our kyé7e helped us develop a basic understanding of Secwepemctsín, since she always gave us the commands of daily living in our language (e.g., dig some potatoes, feed the visitors, pack some water).

She always had strong connections with her extended family; she raised her nephew, Kenny Dennis, from when he was a baby to the day that he was taken to the residential school at four years of age. How heartbreaking that must have been for her. She would often visit his dad and her only brother at Ciyala, her first home. She also visited friends and relatives in Splatsin and Sxwetsmellp, always telling us not to forget our people. She still had the time to take care of her former mother-in-law, who came to live with us until she died, even though she was busy helping our mother, Rita, take care of her nine children.

The fall time was busy when our kyé7e and family worked together to catch salmon to dry in the smokehouse by the river. Everyone I spoke with as I was writing this piece remembers berry picking with her as a child. The summer, when the huckleberries were ready to pick, was one of the best times of the year. As adults, her grandchildren and great-grandchildren continue the tradition of berry picking.

It was through our food gathering that we developed a strong connection to the land, water, and family. This connection to the land included Minnie's second home at Celewt. When visiting there during our annual Mother's Day camp, she would reminisce about the old days, about the garden they'd had, about the dances in the old house, about the horses, about the people who lived at Celewt, and about how she missed them. She would be so happy to know that some of her grandchildren continue the connection to Celewt by building conventional, alternative, and winter homes there. She would also be so happy to know that Janice is one of the many people who have been working tirelessly to revive our language and the ways of our people.

Our kyé7e was definitely a strong and resourceful Secwépemc woman. Despite the fact that she didn't attend school for very long, she learned how to read the newspaper. She survived epidemics, a fractured hip, and many losses, including that of her only grandson. We remain forever grateful for our kyé7e Minnie for the lessons she taught us, her loving care, and the strength she gave us to survive and thrive as a strong Secwépemc family.

JACQUELINE JONES was born in Secwepemculecw. She is one of nine grandchildren of the late Minnie Dick and Sandy Adrian. Her mother, Rita Dick, was also from Secwepemculecw, and her father, Patrick, was from Quebec. She married Truman Jones from the Syilx Nation and has three children. She was fortunate to have been raised by fluent Secwépemc speakers and thus to have developed a basic understanding of her language at an early age. In her career as a registered nurse, she has had the good fortune to work with fluent speakers who helped her develop her understanding and use of Secwepemctsín. Her goal is to continue her learning so that she can pass her knowledge on to her family and her community.

Joseph Stanley Michel with his National Aboriginal Achievement Foundation Award for Education. | *From the private collection of Dr. Kathryn Michel. Photographer unknown*

Joe Stanley Michel (1929–2009)
attended KIRS 1938–1950

Anna Michel teaching students from Chief Atahm immersion school. | *Chief Atahm School*

Anna Michel (b. 1931)
attended KIRS 1940–1951

REMARKS BY PAUL F. MICHEL AND DR. KATHRYN A. MICHEL,
CHILDREN OF JOE AND ANNA MICHEL

On May 27, 2021, we heard there would be an announcement later that day that 215 unmarked graves had been detected by radar at the Kamloops Indian Residential School site. The news was horrifying and tragic but, unfortunately, not shocking. As children of parents who attended the school, we had heard enough stories to sense the magnitude of the traumas and abuses experienced there. In Celia Haig-Brown's book *Resistance and Renewal*, our parents, Anna Michel (Yelqotkwe) and the late Joe Stanley Michel (Cicwelst) shared some of their experiences at the school. When we read their stories, we knew that they had only told the parts they were able or willing to share. Although our parents lived their lives in the shadow of shame and of hurtful, horrifying memories, our father would only talk about his positive experiences at KIRS—his role as advocate, protector, and academic. He would never discuss the abuse he suffered, and ultimately, he took his secrets with him when he passed away. Our mother's memories of the school were often sanitized as a form of self-preservation. She mostly says, "Residential school was good, and it taught us to speak English and to get good jobs." However, sometimes she would share that every time she returned to the school and stared at the white ceilings, "It was like a knife piercing my heart." As children of two residential school survivors, we are acutely aware of the struggles our parents went through and that in many respects, their silence was in fact resilience. We are fortunate that their resilience propelled them to do more than just survive, as they became respected leaders in education and shared their knowledge of Secwépemc culture and language with others.

The primary importance of resistance was to survive the residential school; the secondary mission was to shed the negative influences of those early horrors and abuses. Both our parents lived their lives in duality; they were hindered early in life by shameful thoughts of "being Indian." At the school, they were strongly encouraged to embrace the safety of assimilation by moving away from their old ways. In many respects, they were the poster children of assimilation. Our father became an accomplished teacher, counsellor, and community leader. And our mother's dream of having all nine of her children graduate high school was more than fulfilled when eight out of the nine went on to complete university degrees. As children, we all understood the "role" we were to play in society and that sacrifices had been made by our parents' generation to make our way easier. Unfortunately, the children of the survivors of Indian residential schools also had to overcome shame, violence, and negativity in their own struggles of resistance and renewal.

Although we have each taken different paths—one as Special Advisor to the President on Indigenous Matters at Thompson Rivers University, the other as a professor teaching the Secwépemc language—we both have witnessed the power of resistance and have experienced the healing of renewal. Some in our family have found a path through their careers and through giving back to others, some through finding their identities as Secwépemc through language, songs, stories, and traditions. Our parents once again helped lead the way by devoting their retirement years to teaching the language, stories, and teachings to hundreds of children attending Chief Atahm School, a Secwépemc immersion school started in 1991. Through their role as Elders, we were finally able to see all sides of them. Their talents as storytellers, singers, historians, and teachers were no longer hidden. Without a doubt, renewal of our Secwépemc language, our connections to our land, and to each other are the keys to survival.

On the anniversary of *Resistance and Renewal*, which chronicled the experiences of thirteen KIRS survivors, we, as children of survivors, would like to attest that resistance is a continuous process and that renewal is not only possible, but imperative. The book foreshadowed the tragedy of the unmarked graves, which exposed decades of abuses. It is within such tragedies that we need to find our strength to move forward as a way of honouring the innocent lives lost.

PAUL F. MICHEL belongs to the Secwépemc Nation and is traditionally from Cstélen (Adams Lake First Nation). Paul is honoured to be working as Special Advisor to the President on Indigenous Matters at Thompson Rivers University, and he recognizes that this wonderful university is situated in the traditional territory of Tk'emlúps. Paul has broad-based Indigenous experience in the areas of administration, student support services, university instruction, Indigenous research, and governance.

DR. KATHRYN A. MICHEL writes, "I am a Secwepemc woman. I weave my identity around my land, my Nation, and my family. My journey has led me to live my life working to help revitalize the Secwépemc language through immersion education." Dr. Michel currently teaches the Secwépemc language to babies in the Chief Atahm School language nest and to adults in the Stselxméms r Secwépemc Institute.

Archíe Williams and Julie Antoine, fall 2009. | *Alan Haig-Brown*

Archie Williams (b. 1944) attended KIRS 1952–1959
Julie Antoine (b. 1948) attended KIRS 1953–1962

REMARKS BY JULIE ANTOINE

Kamloops Indian Residential School seems like it just happened yesterday. The memories, the sadness, but most of all the fear about things I done wrong or the hurt I caused to myself will never go away! The last day I was at KIRS, I did not know it was going to be my last day there—that was June 1962. My mom, dad, and grand-mother Susan picked us up—my two brothers, Joseph and Peter, my sisters, Rosalie and Regena, and myself—and our mom and dad was sober! It was a happy moment all the way home to Two Springs! That happiness lasted throughout the summer, and then it was arranged that we would be going to school in Ashcroft, a town that was about forty-five minutes from where we lived. I was overjoyed, bouncing and skipping around like it was awesome! Then the nun, Sister Mary Leonita, tried to get us to go back because KIRS had arranged for our dance group to go to Mexico. That did not inspire me whatsoever, and I was not going back! And I didn't, and today have absolutely no regrets on that decision, because I never ever wanted to go back to that place again. It took away so much of my childhood, my mom and dad, and put all the evil in me that a kid could muster up!

But at home it was not all a happy place neither, because of the drinking, the fighting, the abuse to each other that both parents did. It was an every-weekend occurrence: they seemed to have hated each other. In spite of all that, we still did our gardens, had cattle and horses, summer food gathering, going to the Fraser River to catch and dry salmon to bring home for our winter's food. In the fall we went hunting as a family along with our uncles, aunts, and cousins. That was a fun time, even with the jug of wine that was passed around to the grown-ups. Us kids started sneaking a drink and would often be pretty drunk by the time we got to our camps. Sexual abuse from our grandfather on our dad's side would happen then, not only to us girls, but to the boys too. I finally got brave enough to tell Dad what was happening. That's when he took the ole man, tied him backwards on his horse, and sent him back to his reserve. It stopped in our house until the reserve men knew when our mom and dad would be on a drunk, then they started coming to our house. We learned to hide up in a tree, but a few times they did catch and rape the girls. Throughout our years growing up, we never let them forget what they did; revenge and hate took over our memories. Them men knew how vindictive us girls could be for the rest of their lives. As each died, us girls marked it down—not a good memory, but to us that was payback!

When Archie and I started going together, it was on a dare! People called Archie "Charlie George" after the meanest man in our reserve. People also called him "Little Daddy" because he took charge of his family. A funeral was taking place, and Archie was a pallbearer; he needed someone to hold his cowboy hat, and because of a dare, I reached and grabbed it. He looked and let me take it. Later, when he wanted it back, I said to him, "Why don't we go get a coffee from the Oasis Hotel?" Took a while, but he agreed. We went, had a coffee, talked a little, and he brought me back and I thanked him, made sure my sisters were watching, and went to get my ten dollars from them! I won the bet!

From then on it was Archie and I! I was sixteen years old, and by the time I was eighteen, we were living together. With all my baggage of hate, revenge, bad memories, I never let him talk me down! I could talk like a lumberjack, crude and with lots of anger. Most people just left me alone, just like they did with Archie. When we drank, which wasn't that often, we would fight, then just carry on like it never happened. But alcohol started creeping up more and more with me, and my memories of my childhood started taking over: the hurt, the pain, the sexual abuse, and the hatred was deeper than ever! I had my daughter, Rhoda, when I was eighteen. Archie was wanting to rodeo, but his mom, Bella, came and told us if he was going to rodeo, we had to go as a family, so rodeos, horses, and travelling started. We also got a couple of more kids—our niece and nephew, Rhonda and Keith—and around that time, I had our son, Neal. Three years passed. I drank but not in the open, took care of the kids, still did our winter gathering, canning, fishing, drying, and hunting so we could have our money for rodeos. Then one rodeo the stock contractor needed a timer, and that became my job at every rodeo after that. There were times that I drank, still looked after the kids, did the timing of the events at the rodeo, and thought I could handle all of it. But the memories crept up more and more. Soon I was drinking to be drunk. Archie would take care of the kids. He would get angry with me and tell me to smarten up. I tried but it would get worse.

Finally, I got a job washing dishes at the Oasis Hotel in Cache Creek. That lasted for about two months. They soon found out I could multi-task, cook, and was good at handling money, and I got moved to the cafeteria. I was in my glory. I could talk to people, or rather, ask the tourists where they were from, where were they going, and listen to their woes! That's when Bella, my mother-in-law, had called the Indian agent come to see me. I didn't know until he came to the cafeteria—not even Archie knew. Bella introduced me to him, Cecil Buckley, told him what I did with the tourists and told him, "There must be some kind of school she can take so she can make a job out of her curiosity." She told him how I helped the people before they get on the next bus to carry on to their destination! That was September 1979, and by January 1980, I was upgrading at Kamloops, staying with Archie's cousin Katherine and her husband, Luke. I finished upgrading, got my GED, and came home. Drinking was still a problem, but at least I had an outlook on life, so by then we had about seventeen foster children, still were travelling to rodeos, and had a plan! I could handle everybody else's problem, but not mine!

The one thing both Archie and I agreed on was that our kids would never have to go through what we did—residential school, being taken from us, getting whipped, being hungry or cold, or sexual abuse. But we didn't spare them abuse altogether—fighting, alcohol, and downgrading each other. We separated after a big fight where I ended up in hospital and decided enough is enough of the abuse, but it didn't slow me down on my drinking. My demons where still there, drunk or sober, that followed me. Remembering that my dad didn't even put my name on his goodbye letter he wrote before he committed suicide really took a toll. That was 1976.

One day as I was sobering up, we were at Quilchena Rodeo. I remembered making a fool of myself at the bar the night before. A friend came up to me and asked if I needed an eye-opener. I looked at him and said, "No, thank you!" That was the first time I started facing my demons! From then on it was one day at a time! I enrolled to get an interview to be a teacher at NITEP—that didn't pan out because the interview was going to happen at KIRS! Demons came back with a vengeance. As I told the students that I talked to at the school in Cache Creek recently, NITEP was located in the former senior girls' dormitory of the school. I went up the stairs to the interview as an adult, but by the time I got to the top, I was reduced to that little abused and lonely girl, and I turned around and went straight down the stairs and out the door. So, for about two weeks I was drunk, feeling sorry for myself. My kids were totally disgusted with me, as I was when I sobered up. Here again I let myself down!

Why can't I move on, get rid of this stuff—but how? Then I met with Jack Kakakaway, who was the drug and alcohol worker for Bonaparte. He was needing some furniture because he was moving into an apartment downtown so he could be closer to his job. We had an extra bed, so we took it down to him. Then my journey began. I enrolled in the Native Human Service Program for two years. There I learned about myself, my demons, my triggers, and started a new road. I got to know myself and how to move forward, make steps, make small plans, and live day by day. From there I carried on to be a Drug/Alcohol Counsellor, then went to Sexual Abuse Counselling training, then decided to round it out with Employment Counselling. That was 1984.

By 1985 my relearning of our culture and traditions, our heritage, our family, was important. I then started helping not only myself, but other people. My employment with our band was the most challenging and the most rewarding job I'd ever done. I was the D/A Counsellor for ten years. I even faced and helped clients who were our childhood abusers with their issues. In whatever counselling position I have done, I remembered that I was there once, and everybody needs someone to believe in or some help in their healing journey. So, for the last thirty-eight years, my family takes each step with me. I became a grandmother in 1986, and with Archie and I back together, we made a pact that we would talk it out, we would include our family, and we would not step in front or walk behind, but walk together in all we do. Our family is our number one, we support one another and still rodeo as a family just as Bella, Archie's mom, said we should! We have eight grandchildren and four great-grandchildren! I know now how to take care of the demons! One day at a time!

Archie Williams and Julie Antoine, March 2022. | *Harley Antoine*

JULIE CECILE ANTOINE: My parents were Joe Vance Zabotel, raised in the St'at'imc (Lillooet) Nation and later registered at Bonaparte First Nation, and Anastasia (Alex) Zabotel from the Leon Creek First Nation (Pavilion First Nation). I was raised at a place called Butterfly Springs and lived in a tent the first four years of my life. Then my dad built a house at Two Springs, which is located on the Bonaparte First Nation, Indian Reserve #1.

I married Archie Antoine Williams (Bonaparte First Nation). His parents were Archie Antoine (grandfather: Wilbur Williams, grandmother: Rosie [McLean]) and Bella [Porter] Antoine (grandmother: Julia [Burk] Porter, grandfather: Nels Porter from the Swinomish Tribe, Washington state). We have two children, Rhoda Antoine (married to Carey Isnardy) and Neal Antoine (married to Michelle Haller-Antoine), with eight grandchildren and four great-grandchildren. We raised our nieces, Rhonda Zabotel and Veronica Thomas, and our nephew, William Keith Zabotel, along with seventeen foster children.

Sobriety came in 1984 for myself and in 1986 for Archie. I am a retired Addictions and Employment Counsellor and now do cultural and traditional teachings, along with the use of medicinal plants, at our local schools. Being married to Archie meant that we lived the cowboy/rodeo way of life, as he is a third-generation cowboy; his grandfather Nels Porter was a saddle bronc rider in the early 1900s. His uncle David Perry taught Archie to rope, work the ranch life, and be a "pickup man," as Dave was a rodeo stock contractor who took on Archie to be his helper. In 1974 and also in 1979, while working with Grasslands Rodeo, Archie was voted by his peers to pickup at the first Canadian Finals Rodeo in Edmonton, Alberta. Archie has won five team-roping championships and was inducted in the Cowboy Hall of Fame in 2013. Our children and grandchildren are following in our footsteps in rodeos, being pickup men, and living a cultural and traditional way of life.

To Celia: I read the book again, and this time I really heard the stories. I really had a good cry. Now I see what my mother went through also, because she went from 1931 to 1939, but never ever spoke about that school! Going through some of her papers, she wrote down that she had to live with her aunt when she came home, and her life wasn't so good. Even though she passed in 1986, I had a long talk to her about my life, her life, and finally said I thought she did an awesome job with all of us. And thanks to my grandmother, Susan (her mom), for all her teachings and for not giving up on all of us! I think now we can both move on!

Maria Myers. | *Linda R. Smith*

Maria Myers (b. 1957) attended KIRS 1965–1966, and before that attended St. Joseph's Mission Residential School in Williams Lake

REMARKS BY MARIA MYERS

I am a survivor of the Kamloops Indian Residential School and St. Joseph's Mission Residential School at Williams Lake. The school records there were never properly kept. Those records with mistakes after mistakes followed me to every school, obliterating the fact that I had already attended school for three years, starting when I was six. The records made it seem like I took the same modules three times. There are times when I think maybe I actually did take three years to do one grade. Maybe I was too Tsilhqut'in with an accent and didn't learn my lessons properly. What I would like to think is that I was too Tsilhqut'in for them, and they did not even know what I had learned.

One of the memories that never leaves me is that when I arrived at the residential school, I was sick with the mumps. Some time after our arrival, I remember it being very dark, and I was hurting from the mumps. I looked out the window and remembered my mom. I started crying quite loudly, and no one came. I saw a child with the same sickness not very far from my bed and felt much better because I was not alone. Another memory that sticks in my mind is a boy who had TB, throwing up blood. I spent ten months of the year separated from my family. It was a lonely childhood journey. Our family, upon leaving the school, were not close anymore. We were strangers to each other and not a close-knit group. That outcome was intentional on the part of the nuns and priests who ran the mission school.

The church especially caused us to see our parents as sinners who would burn in hell. Being young, I believed the priest who yelled these words from the pulpit. During Mass, I was so hungry, I would shake from not eating. This had been going on for quite a while; I would attend Mass early in the morning without eating. I had low blood sugar levels, and I would start trembling, kneeling at the pews, and feeling nauseous. I had one nun help me get up, and she told me to sit and hold my head between my legs. I had the shakes like that twice at the Kamloops and St. Joseph's residential schools. I thought my shaking was because I was a sinner.

I was so malnourished that I would resort to stealing bread or apples from the kitchen. Other students would get dried fish and dried meat from home, but I was not so lucky; protein beats bread and an apple any day. Upon my arrival home, we would have deer and moose meat and garden crops to eat. Home was a source of good food, which strengthened me.

I have worked now for a little more than forty years teaching my Tsilhqut'in language to elementary, high school, and adult students. I saw the change when fluent speakers came to the residential schools and slowly started speaking English. The residential schools mocked us for speaking the language and outright forbade it. Making us white Indians is what they intended; the priest and nuns had this as a goal. Now with a resurgence of pride and the healing of time, people are feeling a strong need to learn the language. With help from some outsiders, we in the Tsilhqut'in Nation are trying to meet the increasing demand for classes.

Despite all efforts by the Canadian government and the churches, our culture is still intact. We still live off the land, but now in a more contemporary style. Tsilhqut'in rangers look after the land and the animals. We are doing more work to promote the wellness of our community members, women, and men. The infrastructure on the reserve is improving.

Personally, I have been going to counselling for thirty years or so. I have come a long way from feeling like a victim wherever I went. I joined Hey-way'-noqu' in Vancouver when I was emotionally very low and in need of help. I have verbalized everything that happened to me as a child. I continue to heal with counsellors through art therapy or other counselling methods.

As for my children, they did not go to residential school, but the effects of residential school have carried on to their generation. My grandchildren are at the age that I was in residential school, and they relate to their parents very differently than I did as a child. They are more open, and their family is close-knit. Their parents support their interests in sports, school, and books. They play with the children whenever they can, and I hope they don't ever have to be separated from their family, like I was.

I have continued to think about the church and its role in our lives. Christianity led us to believe in a religion that caused my people to have mixed feelings after the residential school. These mixed feeling caused us to hate words like "sinners," "the devil," and "evil." We may have had similar beliefs, because we have the word "Nentsen" for those things that are bad like "evil" and the "devil." But I like to believe those things were also good in some ways, even though there might have been things to be afraid of in our spirituality.

I am now at a stage in my life where I have said my goodbyes to the church. I do not like what the residential school staff did to my people. I still believe in the Creator and would like to learn more about how we were when there were no white people around. I know there were sweats, both ceremonial and cleansing. I know that with our stories, we had rules, life rules. Why didn't the priests see that and leave us alone? I am tapping into our traditional laws through stories. Our belief in deyen is still here, but I don't hear of very many traditional healers. There are some coming up, but not enough of them. I hear from my mom that her father and mother were healers, and my dad's mom and father were too. It wasn't very long ago that we spiritually lived the old ways with added Christianity. It should probably not be too hard to retrieve what was once our own spirituality.

MARIA MYERS: I am from Yuneŝit'in Band, one of the six Tsilhqut'in Bands. I was born in Yanah in the cold spring weather. My parents frequented the place every summer for summer haying. I love the meadow where I went every summer and winter—in the winter, that is, before I went to residential school. My mother was a monolingual Tsilhqut'in speaker, and my dad was dominant in the Tsilhqut'in language. We had our grandfather living with us sometimes, and he would speak mostly Tsilhqut'in at home. With those three in the household, most of us learned to speak Tsilhqut'in, and we learned English at the residential school. I have made it my life's work to teach the Tsilhqut'in language. I am still at it now, for more than forty years.

Yuneŝit'in language teacher Maria Myers teaching Yuneŝit'in Language Apprentices about pitch making at Yuneŝit'in ʔEsgul, May 2019. Left to right: Brittney Hink, Skyann Setah, and Maria Myers. | *Paula Laita, Yuneŝit'in Language Team*

SPEECHES TO THE PRIME MINISTER OF CANADA, OCTOBER 18, 2021

Charlotte Manuel (b. 1942) attended KIRS in 1959 and later worked in the KIRS kitchen

SPEECH BY CHARLOTTE MANUEL

I carry this stick for all the children of the four directions. I was honoured this stick by Carman McKay when I was teaching young children how to sing and dance and storytell. This is walking eagle. He likes to come out and enjoy everything. He always looks around. This is how I work with the children with this stick. So I carry it and honour them. But first of all I want to lay tobacco down and have a moment's silence for all the children all across Canada and the US, wherever our children were buried by the schools and wherever they were discovered or recovered or found. Okay? So, a moment's silence while I lay tobacco for the children, please.

Kukwstsétselp. I offer tobacco so that we can start in our homes to break the cycles of abuse that come from the residential school, so that we can let go of addictions, that great havoc in our homes and our communities. I offer tobacco for all the children of the four directions so that we can all walk in peace together with each other and start that healing process, because we really need it for our people, and our children who are yet to come. I honour children, and I love children. I have lots of grandchildren, and the biggest thing—and I am very sincere and honest about this, we really need to feel this in our hearts, in our homes—is to bring love back into it. Bring our Creator back into our homes and our communities. But the biggest gift is the gift of forgiveness to ourselves, and everything else will fall into place for others who need to be forgiven. That is the gift that the Creator of all gave to us: the gift of forgiveness. Because if he didn't give us that gift of forgiveness, none of us would be standing here today. And I sincerely honour that gift of forgiveness. My children have taught me how to love myself. When I left that school up there, I didn't know how to love myself. I didn't know how to love my children. My five children taught me how to love them. Thank God for my grandmother. She went to school up here. Thank God for my mother, my auntie—they took me under their wing and raised me. They brought me back to my Native spirituality, and that's what I believe in today. No disrespect to what other people believe, because I was taught to respect what other people believe by my auntie, my mum, and my grandmother.

I was lost when I left from there. Very lost. I didn't know anything. I was confused about what to believe in. I was taught the wrong way to believe in God in that school up there. If it wasn't for my grandmother, my mum, and my auntie, and a few other uncles who came into my life, and also Chief Leonard George. He came up and brought a bunch of runners up here to the school. I was sitting in the chair, and he walked by and he blessed each one of us. He came to me, and he made me stand up and I looked him right in the eyes. He put his hand on my head and on my shoulders and he said, "Now you have your Native spirit, your Indian spirit back in with you," he said. "I called it back for you."

And now today, I am a proud Secwépemc woman. Forty-two years of working on myself in sobriety, in well-briety. I've worked hard on myself. I made lots of mistakes in my life. I own them. Nobody takes the blame for them. I blame myself for them, but I have learned to forgive myself for blaming myself for making mistakes. And I pray that we can have it our hearts to start forgiving and start working and making the truth and reconciliation a path for all of us. For the children of the future. For the children of the past. For the children of now, the present. Let us start with that. Please. I am available anytime you need me; I will come out, and I will help. And that is what I am doing. I am sitting on the thirteen families. I enjoy going to those meetings. I go Tuesday, Wednesday. Tuesday, we have drumming circle, bringing that culture back into the community. I enjoy it. Wednesday, we go do recording, and we have lots of fun when we get together. One day I broke down, and I had a meltdown right in front of the group. They sat there and let me cry because they knew I was hurting, and after we finished they all came and gave me a hug.

So, I believe in my Native spirituality simply because I got married in church and the church told me, you don't belong in here anymore. I said, "Okay, fine." I couldn't understand why the church wouldn't allow me to go to church, so I left and went back to my Native spirituality, and since then I have been happy, and my heart has been filled with a lot of belief. Our Native spirituality does exist—believe me, it does. The ceremonies are still taking place. And be strong: walk your talk and talk your walk and believe in yourself.

I am a proud Secwépemc woman and I say Kukwstsétselp, kel kupik7, Kukwstsétselp, kel kupik7, Kukwstsétselp, kel kupik7. All my relations, ho, ho.

CHARLOTTE FAUSTINE PATRITIA MANUEL: I am eighty years old. I am from the Secwépemc qelmúcw Tk'emlúps. I have learned the roles of the old ones from the wise old ones. Some are here still teaching us, yet some have passed on to the spirit world. May they all rest in peace. I, as an old one in the Tk'emlúps Secwépemc qelmúcw, now carry on the teachings passed on to me from the old wise ones to the young ones from our Tk'emlúps village. When called out to the village to help others, I focus on listening to your body as you age, healing and preparing yourself for the coming changes in life. I want people to enjoy every age, to seek new wisdom, and to move to a sober future one day at a time.

Speaking Notes by Vicki Manuel, daughter of Charlotte Manuel

TO: Mr. Trudeau PM

FROM: Intergenerational Survivor Vicki W. Manuel

Weyt-kp (hello to many) Elders, Chief, Council, Prime Minister, visiting leadership, and community.

Any words I speak are not intended to harm or hurt anybody. This is my truth as an intergenerational survivor.

Since the age of five I feel like I have been in survivor mode, and I am fifty-three years old now, and Prime Minster, I am tired.

I was raised by my mom and, throughout my life, other family members. I am the youngest of five children. I have three older brothers and one older sister.

My mom went to residential school; my three oldest siblings went to day school here at KIRS. By the time my brother Kirby and I were old enough to go to school, it closed. But we still experienced the atrocities imposed onto my mom, my siblings, and other family members in other ways.

We hear about the loss of culture and the loss of our language, but as children growing up in the wake of the residential school era, we lost so much more.

Parenting and Family

- **We lost our parents.** Our moms, our dads, grew up in an institution. A regulated, cold institution that forced them through violence not to have feelings.... Our parents were not able to freely show love or emotions.

- **We lost our ability to know how to parent or to be a parent.** Parented by an institution, our parents were only able to parent with what they knew or were taught at residential school.

- **We lost our father, our dads.** There are no father figures in my family. My mom, myself, my daughters, and granddaughter— four generations without a father figure. Our fathers are lost due to addictions, due to the inability to parent or to know how to parent. They have not done their healing, therefore they have issues establishing positive, respectful, and loving connections.

- **We lost our siblings.** As children, my siblings and I were separated to live among different family or community members. As a little girl I had to leave my brothers and sister, who were my security blanket, who were my best friends, who were my protectors.

Childhood

- **As children we lost a safe, secure, and loving childhood.** Our childhood was filled with violence, addictions, and poverty. Wondering where we were getting our next meal and wondering if we could eat just potatoes for another month. Wondering if the butter knife in the door frame was enough to keep us safe from the predators on the other side. Growing up in a violent environment fuelled by alcohol.

- As children we became the adult, forced to grow up fast, forced to provide for ourselves, to survive and be safe. We became the parents we did not have.

Emotions

- **We lost our ability to have feelings except anger, and there was a lot of ANGER.** We grew up in environments where feelings were not acceptable. We were not to show any weaknesses and absolutely no tears. We were taught to compress and stifle all our feelings.

Alcohol and Addictions

- **We lost our loved ones to addictions, and in my family, they are lost to alcohol.** In 2012 my nephew shot himself in the head. He had what I call liquid courage (alcohol) to help him pull the trigger. Four months later my dad died of cirrhosis of the liver. The other day I went and picked up my brother from detox for the third time this year. We pray that this time he calls his spirit back and he heals.... My other brother is dying a slow death as he continues to battle the bottle on a daily basis. Our youth are experiencing the same alcoholic addictions among other drug addictions, and this worries me as a mom.

Sexual Abuse

- **We lost our innocence to sexual abuse.** The sexual abuse our families experienced at residential school then crept into our communities, and all innocence was lost. As such we became hypervigilant, anxious, and always afraid.

Death and Grief

- We rarely experience our family members dying of a natural cause (old age). Our deaths are from addictions, overdoses, violence, suicides, chronic health conditions, and poverty.

Sense of Self

- Growing up we lost our sense of self. Going to town to attend a public school during the daytime and then coming back home to the rez ... two totally different worlds, and in each trying to find our way, how we fit, and who we are. Mostly just trying to survive and avoid the racism we felt at school.

Shame

- We learned how to SHAME each other from the residential school. The residential school was successful in instilling SHAME into who we are and then teaching us how to SHAME each other.... This is not our Secwépemc way, to Shame, but one that we have inherited and are working on to rid.
- **The children resting in the sacred burial ground lost the ability to live their life—I feel it is our duty to live our best life in their memory....**
- **As much as we need to speak of the losses, the trauma the grief, I feel it is just as important to speak to our success and to leave you with a message of HOPE ...**

Mom—My púsmen (heart)

- Mom has been clean and sober for forty-two years.
- She is helping to bring back our Secwépemc songs and dances.
- My mom has taught me that it is okay to have and experience all feelings and emotions ... and that I am safe.

- My mom has an open-door policy and a revolving door for my children and I, but also to anybody in our community who needs an ear, a hug, a brushing off, or a safe place.
- My mom has lived in violence, been shamed, punished, but has healed, is healing, and has, in her healing journey, learned how to forgive. My mom is my hero.

Me

- I walk in two worlds: the Western world and the Secwépemc world (with my culture and my teachings grounding me in both).
- I have two university degrees under my belt.
- I have served on council for my community for six years.
- I single-parented three amazing, kind, intelligent, and beautiful daughters—all three have graduated.
- My home is a safe and loving space, and there is always food in the fridge.
- I continue to heal.
- And most importantly—I KNOW WHO I AM.

I come from a long line of STRONG Secwépemc women. Every day, I see sunshine and happiness for my granddaughter. We will continue to walk in two worlds with grace and ferocity, always grounded in our Secwépemc Way of Being. Every day, I pray for the children and our healing.

Thank you

VICKI W. MANUEL (an intergenerational survivor) is a Secwépemc woman from Tk'emlúps te Secwépemc, with three grown daughters (Ashley, Alecia, and Jada) and a granddaughter, Aveah. Vicki and her partner, Peter, live and work in beautiful Tk'emlúps. Charlotte

Manuel (Vicki's mom) passed on the traditional knowledge that grounds Vicki in her everyday life and dealings. Employed as manager of Le Estcwicwéy̓ (The Missing), she has a master's degree in community development from the University of Victoria and served on her band council for six years. Vicki is passionate about her family, planning, and creativity through photography, woodwork, and painting. She is active in seeking ways she can influence communities and systems to be more culturally aware so that her granddaughter's future will be a more inclusive one, with endless opportunities for her to succeed.

Speech by Ashley N. Michel, granddaughter of Charlotte Manuel

Mr. Trudeau, there is a lot I want to say, but you don't know me. My voice may shake a little, and I am crying, but I need you to listen, and I want you to hear my voice. My name is Ashley. I am a proud Indigenous mother, and I come from a long line of strong, independent, successful Secwépemc women.

I am hurting. My heart aches for the mothers who never got to see their babies again. My heart aches for the children who were scared and lonely and just wanted to go home but didn't make it. My heart aches for the children who were robbed of their childhood, culture, language, and traditions, some of whom are sitting around you here today. Because of what happened, because of residential schools and the forced assimilation, colonization, and genocide of our people on Turtle Island, I am mourning for our language, culture, and traditions, which I am so desperately trying to reclaim and teach my daughter before it's too late. I want a good life and future for her and the future generations to come. A good future means a life where she is not grieving, where she is not triggered. Our kids do not need to feel this pain, and it stops with my generation.

I want our children to have a future where their voices are heard. Where they don't have to worry about being another statistic. Where our people are safe and the crisis of the Missing and Murdered Indigenous Women, Girls, Trans, and Two-Spirit People is no more. Where our children have clean drinking water. Where they don't have to defend their sacred traditional land. Where our children are not removed from their families and communities and placed in care. Where Indigenous mothers can have their babies peacefully without worrying their newborn child will be taken away. Where our children can successfully walk in two worlds and practise our culture, traditions, and language and have healing. After everything, our babies, the missing, deserve to be found, identified, and brought home.

Our children deserve a good future, and our families deserve peace. So how do we get there? We need more than words and broken promises, Mr. Trudeau. We need action, we need justice, and we need accountability. Listen and learn from our Elders and survivors while they are still here. Ask for their knowledge and advice to move us on a path forward. Use your power and privilege for good. And make this visit count.

Kukwstsétselp.

ASHLEY N. MICHEL: Weyt-kp, my name is Ashley Michel. I am Secwépemc from Tk'emlúps Indian Band, and I have a beautiful daughter named Aveah. My mother is Vicki Manuel. My father is Paul Michel. My two grandmothers are Charlotte Manuel and Floral Sampson, both of whom are residential school survivors.

Four generations: Charlotte Manuel, daughter Vicki, granddaughter Ashley, and great-granddaughter Aveah embrace after the speeches. | *Jennifer Gauthier/Reuters*

Closing Note

The strength of Indigenous culture is evident in the ways that the survivors in this study dealt with the institution of residential school by successfully resisting its interventions in their lives. Despite the odds against them, despite the illness and repression around them, despite the deaths of so many students, somehow, they survived. Even as they rejected the goal of assimilation, they also found ways to adopt aspects that appeared worthwhile and refuse the others.

With the strength of family, of other students, and of themselves, the survivors refused to comply fully with the oppressors' efforts to dictate their lifestyles. Some adapted the invaders' lifestyle to their own way of being. Catholicism was combined with Indigenous spirituality, and the English language was accepted, but Indigenous languages were never completely repressed. Traditions, teachings, and customs passed on through generations were maintained. Indigenous people resisted; Indigenous ways of being in the world survived and remain as constantly rising forces for action and change within a self-defined Indigenous context.

The residential school is closed. The buildings, now owned by the Tk'emlúps te Secwépemc, are the site of ever-increasing Secwépemc-controlled activity. People can justly celebrate this expression of the indomitable human spirit. The people who agreed to tell their stories in this book are all survivors. Although many continue to work to heal from the impacts of residential school, at the same time, they contribute to the renewal of their ways of life in innumerable ways. As parents and grandparents, teachers and students, politicians and band executives, entrepreneurs and rodeo champions, they define Indigenous cultures in their vibrant and evolutionary state. In the words of Rita Jack, former administrator of the Secwepemc Cultural Education Society,

> The legacy of the residential school experience is that we now have generations of Shuswap people who, not by their own choice, are unable to participate in the academic education of their children. In order to best plan for the future educational needs of Shuswap children, it is necessary to acknowledge the present situation.... We need once more to make education a priority in communities. (1985, 9)

Always remembering the past, people engage in dialogue with one another in the present to create a different future. The strength that resisted the onslaught of cultural invasion perpetrated by the residential school for almost a century is the strength of a people and a nation which continues to survive and grow.

Study Notes

This work began its life as a master's thesis in curriculum and instruction at the University of British Columbia. For those who want to follow the path that led me to this work, three sections follow. First a brief look at my connection to and interest in this topic and how it informed my commitment to respectful research. Second, some ideas that shaped my thinking, including Paolo Freire and my commitment to working against bias in the written record about residential schools available at the time of the research. Finally, a section on how Indigenous educational policy played out in British Columbia after residential schools, highlighting some of the ongoing colonial strategies, as well as Indigenous resistance and creativity. This section can be ignored by those who came to the book primarily for the stories told by the people who attended KIRS.

1. RESEARCH JOURNEY

While I came to this research in 1985, my interest had been sparked by conversations with friends over many of the previous years. The strength of what resulted is directly related to the time we spent together long before there was any suggestion that the stories we told each other would become first a master's thesis, then a book, and now another version of that book. If there is any lesson to be learned from the path we have followed together, it is that building respectful and, I would go so far as to say, loving relationships can only happen over time.

In a 1985 article, Valerie Polakow elaborates on the importance of storytelling in conducting research with often marginalized groups in society whose voices have been ignored and undermined—the invaded and the oppressed. Her article points out that too much educational research, based as it is in social science, has been an attempt to emulate the so-called true sciences.

> In contemporary social science, stories are often deemed as soft—
> they do not constitute the real data of the scientific enterprise....
> The isolation of body, of mind, of experience, of consciousness
> leads to documentation, to a mere taxonomy of facts closed in on
> themselves, leading us away from, not towards, the understand-
> ing of human experience. (826)

Decrying this approach to research, she goes on to point out the importance of storytelling as a form of research. The careful selection of stories by the researcher, who "is an embedded participant, not a distant, uninvolved observer of the humanscope" provides the key to storytelling as sound human science research.

WHY THIS RESEARCH?

I began the formal research for this study of the Kamloops Indian Residential School as what scholars might call an informal partici-pant observer involved in "the process of living." My involvement with Indigenous people in the Kamloops area spanned a period of fifteen years. Originally, as a teacher in two of the secondary schools,

I worked with some Indigenous students in my classes. Another intense connection was through Grasslands Rodeo Company, where I was fully involved in rodeo production. A number of Indigenous people in the Kamloops area have lifetime commitments to rodeo. Over the years I developed strong friendships with some of the rodeo people. In 1976, I moved formally into the field of Indigenous education through my work as coordinator of the Kamloops site of the Native Indian Teacher Education Program (NITEP, now the Indigenous Teacher Education Program[9]), an alternative program offered by the University of British Columbia (UBC) for prospective elementary teachers. In this capacity, I served as teacher, counsellor, seminar leader, and practicum supervisor, working with Indigenous adults. I mention these involvements because they provided the basis for long-term, trusting relationships with people. The friendships served as the starting point which, when accompanied by an explanation of the work I was doing, enabled me to return to informal conversations we had had about an emotion-filled area. In my role with NITEP, as my knowledge of Indigenous people's histories and social circumstances grew, the importance of the persisting impacts of the residential school and the lack of documentation of it became ever clearer to me. The interviews provided an opportunity for us to focus on an area of concern and significance for many Indigenous people of the Kamloops area.

Only with the direct involvement—the words—of the people in the presentation of history can a non-Indigenous person do justice to Indigenous perspectives. Through their words in this text, the residential school that lives in the memories of the participants takes shape before our eyes. The cultural invasion, the resistance

9 See https://nitep.educ.ubc.ca/.

to this invasion, and ultimately, the ongoing cultural and linguistic renewal and overall survivance of a group of people in the central Interior of British Columbia are revealed.

As I took on the role of coordinator of NITEP, a strong sense of irony focused my attention on the stories of the former students of KIRS. Originally the KIRS senior girls' dormitory, the top floor of the east side of the huge brick building completed in 1923 now houses the NITEP centre in Kamloops. Frequently, students coming to be interviewed for admission or their first class said to me very calmly, "My bed was right by that window," or by that door, or around that corner. And the stories began to pour forth—stories of loneliness, pain, camaraderie, and resilience. The irony that I saw came with the people who had returned to school, to what had been a place filled with painful memories, to study to be teachers. They came by choice as mature students with the clear goal in mind to create better learning spaces for the children—how different from the other times.

The Kamloops Indian Band (now Tk'emlúps te Sewépemc) owns the buildings which were the Kamloops Indian Residential School. As I have discussed earlier, within these buildings, educational activities from historical research to curriculum development and many more are all in progress. They have the potential to affect and have already affected the school lives of the community children. In order to appreciate this phenomenon as a tremendous expression of the survival of a culture and a group of people, I wanted to delve into the history that led to the present state. Beneath the surge in educational activity lay almost a century of formal schooling for the most part dominated and controlled by religious and governmental policies established unilaterally by European society.

INTERVIEWING

I began my formal research examining written material as a way to understand something of the attitudes and ambitions that guided the people who established and controlled the residential school. Records at the Public Archives of British Columbia, Oblate Provincial House in Vancouver, the Secwépemc Museum and Archives, and the libraries at Cariboo College (now Thompson Rivers University) and UBC provided a brief but basic picture of the European perspective. That total cultural annihilation was the goal of governments and missionaries is immediately evident in the written records. That these efforts to assimilate Indigenous people were on the whole successfully resisted became the ultimate focus of the people's stories.

Because the stories so vividly depicted life in the residential school—frequently in a very different light than the written records suggested—I decided interviewing would be the most satisfactory approach to presenting some of the history of the school from former students' perspectives. Thirteen intensive one- to two-hour interviews formed the kernel of the material included. In addition, I kept field notes on more casual discussions with numerous other Indigenous people. Interviews were taped and transcribed. Because two participants did not want to be taped, I made notes during the interviews with their agreement. I was particularly interested in facets of school life that were deemed contrary to values and beliefs held before coming to school; in the forms of resistance students developed to the foreign expectations of the people in charge; and finally, in the effects of schooling on the students' relationships with their families when they returned home.

The interviews themselves were very flexible. Though I prepared some general questions beforehand, I rarely referred to them during an interview.

1. Tell me about your involvement with the school. Years? Grades?

2. What were the rules that stood out in your mind?

3. Children often have ways of getting around rules. Did you? Did others? In what ways?

4. Describe your day. What did you do in the classroom? What subjects? How long? Specific lessons?

5. How often did you go home? Where was it? Did your parents visit? Describe visits.

6. Were there aspects of school that contradicted what you were taught at home? What were they?

7. Religion was an important part of school. Was it compatible with what you had learned at home?

8. Did you see friends resisting school? Complying with school?

9. Going home. How was it to go home? Were there adjustments within yourself that had to be made? Did friends or other relatives struggle with going home?

Instead, the flow of the interview was guided by the stories the person wanted to tell, rather than my prepared questions. Without exception, people raised the issues of cultural violation and resistance to that violation. The place of interviewing was most often my office in the residential school buildings. The room itself stirred many memories. "This used to be sister's bedroom," commented one person. On some occasions, particularly when speaking with older people, I went to their homes. My kitchen table was also the site of many tales told by casual visitors about the residential school. Generally, I chose to interview people with whom I already had a relationship, their relatives, or people whom others had suggested as strong storytellers. Those who hesitated when I asked them, I did not interview. I knew that recalling the stories could be harsh and that people had many reasons for not wanting to revisit them. Those who did agree to an interview were made aware that they could end it whenever they chose and that they could refuse to answer any question. Almost without exception, people spoke openly about their school lives. Needless to say, the interviewing I did only scratched the surface.

The accounts reproduced here were generally fuller and more open than is often the case with one-time interviews because, in most cases, I had a prior positive relationship with the person I was interviewing. Their willingness to engage intensely and emotionally as they shared stories of their school lives was based in this pre-established trusting relationship. In some cases where a person had been recommended to me, the fact that we had friends in common made it possible to establish rapport quickly. As a white woman doing this work, my connections with people that had over time allowed them to trust me with their lives were essential. I do not mean to imply in any way that such a relationship can or should be developed in order to interview, but rather the converse. I also acknowledge that since this first formal study, I have engaged in research in places where my relationships with the people there were newer and even non-existent. In those cases, I work to find ways to connect prior to ever seeking permission to conduct research. That way, people have some opportunity to see who I am and how I work before I request permission to conduct research with them.

Some researchers are suspicious of interviews that ask people to recall events from a distant past; they express concerns about the selectivity of memory and the possible distortion of these memories over time. While acknowledging such concerns, I have some thoughts about writing history. Selection of material presented is a problem encountered in any documentation of fact or history. Memories which survive over time in people's minds may be those of the more salient experiences. Rather than seeing time only as distorting, we might also consider it as a filter that allows clearer vision of the matters of importance in a person's life.

As well, I want to emphasize the oral tradition of the Secwépemc people and other Indigenous peoples of the surrounding regions. Unlike some other Indigenous nations in Canada, those in the central Interior of the province did not traditionally transmit culture in written form. As has already been mentioned, storytelling has been the most important means of passing along history and traditions since time immemorial. Even in the now literate culture of the Indigenous nations, the ability to tell stories faithfully is a respected skill. Storytelling continues to be an important dialogical tool for conveying teachings and truths, often in the guise of entertainment. I propose that the long tradition of storytelling—one which includes the retelling of stories many times with little or no change (Teit [1909] 1975, 621)—contributes to accurate presentation of events even long after their occurrence. Maria commented on this notion as it exists in Tsilhqut'in culture: "There is no distinction between telling lies and not remembering or exaggerating. There's no difference; all of them are lies." For her, remembering is a value-laden activity. Closely associated with telling the truth, speaking remembrances is socially acceptable only when it is faithful to the previous accounts.

Notably, since this work was originally published, in the famous 1997
Delgamuukw case, the Supreme Court of Canada accepted both oral
tradition and oral histories as legitimate evidence for legal decision
making.

> Notwithstanding the challenges created by the use of oral histories
> as proof of historical facts, the laws of evidence must be adapted
> in order that this type of evidence can be accommodated and
> placed on an equal footing with the types of historical evidence
> that courts are familiar with, which largely consists of historical
> documents. This is a long-standing practice in the interpretation
> of treaties between the Crown and aboriginal peoples.[10]

The oral histories, people's stories of their experiences within this
book, are finally acceptable evidence in the court system—truths to
be heard.

ANALYZING AND WRITING

As my interviewing progressed and I moved to analysis of what I
had heard, I found my mental image of the school constantly changing. Each new idea expressed produced a slight reshuffling of the
pieces that made up the visualization I was developing of the school.
Occasionally an interview produced so many ideas or an idea of
such import that it was like turning a kaleidoscope; the overall pattern changed radically, incorporating old bits of coloured glass with
new bits to form an entirely new design. These initial reactions to
the interviews were followed by the more comprehensive analysis of

10 *R. v. Sioui* (1990), *supra*, at p. 1068; *R. v. Taylor* (1981), 62 C.C.C. (2d) 227 (Ont. C.A.), at p. 232.; and
Delgamuukw v. British Columbia (1997): https://scc-csc.lexum.com/scc-csc/scc-csc/en/item/1569/
index.do.

the transcriptions of the interviews and a review of the field notes, which included aspects of my changing impressions.

I began to look deeper, with a thorough reading of the transcripts. I marked what I considered to be noteworthy points. On a second reading, I prepared a list of the most striking topics that arose from each interview. These consisted of points I felt would be useful in recreating a representation of the people's perspectives of the school and its effects on them. I had in my mind a general direction in which the information might lead me, but remained open to changes that secondary examination of the interviews might encourage me to emphasize. I found myself thinking most often of a quiltmaker. The people I talked with contributed to the design of each square, and my job was to arrange them in an effective design and to stitch them together to fashion a faithful entity. The stories form our quilt, made of people's strength, resistance, pain, change, and adaptation.

Originally in an effort to maintain the university-required confidentiality of the interviews, I included only minimal details about each person. I assigned each person a pseudonym and a number and included the following details: nation, year of birth, and years of attendance at the school. The analysis for the most part was not arranged chronologically. When I felt that the time of a particular comment was important, I usually indicated a decade. Although many policies changed over the term of the school's operation, outstanding was the commonality of feelings about the school. Some details of daily life changed over time, but the study participants' attitudes to an oppressive and dehumanizing system remained fairly constant.

Because I came to this work as a privileged guest, I felt that it was most important to seek some form of official approval of my work before beginning it. The mandate of the recently formed Secwepemc Cultural Education Society was "to work in unity to: Preserve and Record—Perpetuate and Enhance our Shuswap Language, History and Culture" (Secwepemc Cultural Education Society 1982). Because non-Indigenous people in general and academics in particular had often been rightfully accused of approaching Indigenous nations, peoples, and experiences insensitively and exploitatively, I saw my request to conduct the study as a small way to address this concern directly. With the society's approval, and working closely with society staff and some board members, I felt more confident that my work would not simply be an ethnocentric academic exercise, but it might prove useful to the Secwépemc in the work of providing positive education for their people. I also felt it was important to give the participants an opportunity to comment on my selections from their stories and my speculations regarding what they had shared. I met with the majority of them following the writing of this and reviewed with them the parts of the text where I had used their words. Without exception, they approved the selections I had made and the ways in which I had contextualized them. I wanted to avoid any possibility of misrepresenting what had been said. This sign of my commitment to trying to do research respectfully was emphasized by the importance of my pre-existing relationships. The place of respect in conducting research was reinforced by other ideas that guided my inquiry, which I will discuss below.

2. IDEAS SHAPING THE BOOK

Two ideas that shaped this book in important ways were the thinking of Paulo Freire and the importance of listening to Indigenous people about their experiences in residential schools. Paulo Freire was a Brazilian educator whose ideas strongly influenced the analysis embedded in the earlier chapters of this book. Freire's attention to colonialism and educational policy and practice helped make sense of the importance of schooling and residential schools in the process of colonization or "invasion." In fact, an even earlier version of this book, the thesis itself, was titled "Invasion and Resistance." With my editor's guidance, I moved to resistance and renewal to sharpen the focus on the narratives on Indigenous resistance and survival in the face of the horrors of residential schools, rather than simply on the atrocities of the schools.

Canada as a nation, strong in their beliefs in hierarchy and the superiority of their cultures, attempted in the guise of teachers and priests to annihilate Indigenous cultures and to absorb the children of those cultures into their control under their assumed power structure. Inherent in the notion of hierarchy within capitalism— the driving force of the colonization of North America—is the possibility of rising to a position of superiority, sometimes called meritocracy. Rarely acknowledged by the proponents of this form of capitalism is that this myth allows for only a few in the upper echelons of material wealth and power while the masses struggle among themselves against the hegemony which the system perpetrates. For one to win, the others must lose. In the residential school, the message clearly given to most of the students was that they, because of their history and current circumstances, were inferior.

Anti-dialogical action—action that is based on the desire of one group in society to dominate and control another group through silencing that group—is a focal point of Freire's theories of teaching and learning. He writes of cultural invasion as a phenomenon in which

> the invaders penetrate the cultural context of another group, in disrespect of the latter's potentialities; they impose their own view of the world upon those they invade and inhibit the creativity of the invaded by curbing their expression. (1970, 150)

Schooling, particularly as seen in the residential schools, developed by immigrant Europeans and their descendants for Indigenous people in Canada, has typically been an arm of what Freire calls cultural invasion. As authors of and actors in the invasion, members of the dominating society attempted to mould and act for Indigenous people who, as objects of the invasion, were expected to follow the choices made for them. He goes on to point out that this kind of domination is perpetrated through invasion, whether overt and physical or camouflaged with the invader in the role of the helping friend.

The experiences of the students who attended KIRS, articulated within the text, demonstrate clearly the anti-dialogical nature of the policies which were designed to control their lives. Regardless of intentions, the school experiences that resulted from governmental and ecclesiastical policies most often proved to be of dubious or negative value for the Indigenous children who attended the institution. In almost all cases, the residential school was less successful than anticipated by policy-makers, teachers, and parents alike.

Cultural invasion as discussed and revealed in the stories recounted is one means of imposing a power structure. In this case,

Europeans attempted to impose their hierarchical model upon members of other distinct cultural groups: the Indigenous peoples and nations of the central Interior of BC. The policy-makers and implementers of both the government and the church adhered to the notion of their superiority in dealing with Indigenous children. They believed they knew what was best in almost all regards. Their experiences of life were significant and to be acted upon; the students' experiences were limited, devalued, and dismissed.

CENTRING/LISTENING TO INDIGENOUS VOICES

Another idea that shaped this book was the importance of listening to Indigenous voices. At the time the first edition of this book was completed, although some similar questions had been raised elsewhere in existing literature, little of the writing involved the actual experiences of Indigenous people. Most often, researchers consulted only archival material: letters and diaries written by Europeans about Indigenous people, registers and other reports compiled by Europeans, and reports filed by European church and government officials about Indigenous people. This became especially apparent to me as I searched through archives and libraries for previous works on educational policy and residential schools.

The search yielded a brief survey of the literature tangentially relevant to the 1986 study of the Kamloops Indian Residential School. The works can be broadly categorized into historical, anthropological, and educational studies. Historically, economic, political, and cultural systems originating in Europe have played the major roles in the development of Canada as a nation. Robin Fisher (1977), referring to historians' writing of British Columbia, states that these historians deal with the Indians only as they respond to the European economic system, accommodating to European demands rather than acting in terms of the priority of their own culture. (xi)

Almost without exception, early works showed European perceptions of Indigenous cultures as inferior and primitive (Maclean 1896; Hill-Tout 1907). A strong sense of white superiority, accompanied by a tendency to generalize, to subsume the many and varied nations of Indigenous peoples from across the country or across the province into one amorphous group, led to a hazy view of Indigenous people (Department of Citizenship and Immigration, Indian Affairs Branch 1960; Grant 1984). Because academics writing of Indigenous history had tended to rely primarily on written records for their research, they presented most often the views of the white fur trader, settler, Indian agent, and missionary (Morice [1906] 1978; Cronin 1960; Hewlett 1964; Wilson 1986). By far, the majority of the lengthy quotations were the words of Euro-Canadians; all too rare was attention on the words of Indigenous people. Because few Indigenous people kept written records, interviewing was often the only means of garnering their views of history. With notable exceptions (Berger 1977, 1981; Brody 1981), few researchers writing of (or with?) Indigenous people took the time to develop the trusting and understanding relationships necessary for open communication and meaningful interviews.

Educational writing, like all writing, is shaped by the society within which it is formulated. British Columbia has a pre-Confederation history that refuses to acknowledge the existence of Indigenous people. Unlike other provinces, few treaties dealing with relatively few portions of land were drawn up to address the issue of Aboriginal title. Douglas, the first governor of the colony of Vancouver Island, insisted that

> only after the aboriginal title had been extinguished by treaty could settlement proceed.... The settlers denied that it was their responsibility, and they would not vote funds for the purpose. (Berger 1981, 222–223)

The policy of denying that Aboriginal title had ever existed persisted when the new colony of British Columbia united with Vancouver Island in 1866. Because the provincial government chose to ignore Indigenous people and nations, no consideration was given to their schools. The federal government's assumption of responsibility for "Indians" in 1876 reinforced this attitude. In his 1936 doctoral dissertation, "The History of Education in the Crown Colonies of Vancouver Island and British Columbia and in the Province of British Columbia," Donald MacLaurin, the assistant superintendent of education for BC, does not even mention Indigenous people. As a result of federal control as outlined in the Indian Act, people writing about Indigenous education tended to write about it as a national concern. Reports and research often failed to consider the concerns or perspectives of individual nations, schools, or people, but rather reflected a more generalized national view articulated by the Department of Indian Affairs (DIA).

Leading up to the 1980s, much of the research and publishing on Indigenous education was done under the auspices of the DIA. Materials that embellished the department's image and depicted its successes were more acceptable than those that might lead to hints of racism and perhaps threaten the careers of the elected officials at its head. A book entitled *The Education of Indian Children in Canada* (1965) presents itself as "A symposium written by members of the Indian Affairs Education Division with Comments by the Indian Peoples." It outlines policy decisions and changing legislation. The direct involvement of Indigenous people is found only in the short commentaries that follow each chapter. On the topic of Indigenous involvement in decision making, the closing chapter contains a most revealing statement.

> At present the education of Indian people is directed almost exclusively by outsiders. The federal, provincial and municipal authorities argue, discuss and decide. Indian people participate, but more to ratify than to plan, so is it any wonder that Indians continue to remain unexcited about our program for their education? (Indian Affairs Education Division 1965, 96)

This paradoxical approach continues to the present day: while paying lip service to the involvement of the people in self-determination, those in control simultaneously present plans for ratification. In Freire's words, "The invaders act; those they invade have only the illusion of action, through the action of the invaders" (1970, 150).

A significant and somewhat divergent study from 1967, often referred to as the Hawthorn report, while generalizing as *A Survey of the Contemporary Indians of Canada*, is structured around research with a number of bands across the country. As was the case with many of the historical writings, the credited quotations are those of the white experts: church people, school people, and department people. Generally limited to single words and phrases, Indigenous people's responses to questions regarding the need for education sound shallow and ill-conceived: "Education makes life easier," or

"Education helps you get along with whites better" (Hawthorn 1967, 137). The Indian voices exist only through layers of European interpreters.

Few works on residential schools in western Canada existed in the 1980s. One such study that focused on a Yukon residential school, *The School at Mopass* (King 1967), was thorough and included considerable comment on the school by Indigenous students and workers. The study was commissioned by the Indian Affairs Branch because officials found that the school

> is dysfunctional in the sense that it does not produce the kind of product which it is intended to produce. The desired "product" might be defined as a well-integrated Canadian citizen equipped with attitudes and intellectual skills that enable him to function within the larger society in basically the same manner as other citizens. (ix)

Despite the author's intent not to be influenced by the sponsorship of his study, his ethnocentric bias surfaces in comments such as:

> Those elements [of traditional culture] that linger seem to be a reactive defense mechanism for coping with the powerful but generally apathetic Whiteman society rather than a deliberate or functional persistence of cultural traits as valued entities in themselves. (27)

On the other hand, his criticisms of the school and nearly all portions of society responsible for its inhumanity and ineffectiveness are well taken.

Two articles published separately in BC *Studies* included some interesting insights into residential schools. Coates (1985) relied heavily on archival material, including files of letters from Indigenous people to school officials, to construct his thesis that the school at Carcross in the Yukon "failed to provide the Native students with an obvious route into either native or white society" (47). Redford (1979–1980) summarized attendance statistics to demonstrate the control that Indian parents had over the starting date and the duration of their children's time at residential school. A collection of articles entitled *Indian Education in Canada* (Barman et al. 1986) includes several allusions to residential schools in Canada. Although the emphasis is on archival material as a source of data, it includes notable exceptions, such as the linguistic study by Marie Battiste and the summary of an extensive study by Diane Persson (1980) on the Blue Quills school in Northern Alberta.

Other references to residential schools were found within larger studies. Mary Ashworth (1979) took the time to interview a former residential school student for inclusion as a part of a chapter on the history of Indigenous education in BC. Her use of other Indigenous sources for information led her to the conclusion that Indigenous people must control their own education, an indication of the depth of her understanding of the need to address change in Indigenous education. The historical record, as it existed in the 1980s, was decidedly Eurocentric and felt very disconnected from my experiences working in the vibrant NITEP in Kamloops. This disjuncture between the current written record and my experiences brought a desire and a sense of responsibility to shift the narrative.

LISTENING TO INDIGENOUS VOICES

Archival material can serve as a starting point for research with Indigenous people, but then and now, it benefits from critical questioning and, where possible and practical, direction from Indigenous people themselves. At the time of the original research for this book, the failure to include the words of Indigenous people who had actually experienced the life described in archival documents and other records really was nothing short of absurd when so many were still with us. Residential schools began in British Columbia in the late 1800s. Most closed in the late 1960s. Literally thousands of First Nations people living in the province attended one or another of the schools at some time and had a wealth of information to share. Of course, research approaches are different now, and additional work has been done. In 2020, the research and publications of the Truth and Reconciliation Commission have done exactly what was needed: they listened to those thousands of First Nations people tell their stories of residential school experience and its ongoing impact. Numerous Indigenous authors have written their own stories in the form of novels, poetry, and memoirs.[11]

When former students or their children write of residential school, a significant point recurs within their stories: Indigenous people have consistently resisted the onslaught against themselves and their ways of being in the world. In the first iteration of this book, resistance became a major consideration. I was aware that it had been a focus of study for several educational researchers prior to the 1980s, albeit in other contexts. The most fascinating

11 One list is available here at the time of writing: https://www.cbc.ca/books/48-books-by-indigenous -writers-to-read-to-understand-residential-schools-1.6056204.

aspect of these considerations of resistance were the ways that they led students to produce culture—a culture of resistance within schools as a response to authoritarian control (Apple 1977; Giroux 1981). Whenever such a system existed, an opportunity for resistance to that system was also created. Paul Willis, in his study of working-class youth in an English industrial town (1977), examined the phenomenon of a counter-school culture: "Opposition to the school is principally manifested in the struggle to win symbolic and physical space from the institution and its rules" (260).

This resistance to an oppressive system was paralleled in the Kamloops Indian Residential School. The stories contained in this book and in the works of so many Indigenous authors more recently demonstrate clear defiance of colonial authority, which in turn created a strong community support group among the students. This community spirit not only permitted but actually fostered the survival of a strong Indigenous identity, which was perceived by the students themselves as very different from that of the Europeans who served as teachers and supervisors. Although the residential school indubitably had enormous impact on the lives of all who attended, it failed in its efforts to assimilate Indigenous people into European mainstream society. In the words of the great Secwépemc leader George Manuel, "At this point in our struggle for survival, the Indian peoples of North America are entitled to declare a victory. We have survived" (Manuel and Posluns 1974, 4).

3. TOWARD INDIGENOUS CONTROL

A brief overview of Indigenous education as it played out in British Columbia more generally, both historically and in the 1980s, provides some insights into the developments that now serve as foundation to ever-increasing Indigenous control of Indigenous education, lands, and governance. The struggles at the Kamloops Indian Residential School were struggles for power and control as the European invaders and Indigenous resistance clashed with one another.

THE 1950S AND '60S: SEEKING BETTER SCHOOLS

Although residential schools served as one of the strongest tools used by Euro-Canadians in their efforts to assimilate Indigenous peoples, their closure clearly did not signal an end to the ongoing struggle for cultural recognition and meaningful education by the diverse Indigenous groups in British Columbia and across Canada. After much lobbying by First Nations people, major revisions to the Indian Act in 1951 included the option for "Indian" children to attend public schools. In Canada, "Indians" are under the jurisdiction of the federal government, and education falls within provincial jurisdiction. Funding agreements between individual school districts in BC and the federal government made throughout the decade were eventually formalized and generalized as the Master Tuition Agreement (MTA). Negotiated solely between the federal and provincial governments with no input or oversight by First Nations, it was a bone of contention among First Nations people for many years. It did, however, allow for the attendance of First Nations children in the public school system for a fee. Non-Indigenous children were entitled to free public education. This move to the MTA was expected to serve as the answer to First Nations educational needs. With little overt consideration of the effects of integrating the schools, apparently those involved assumed that teaching the same content in the same ways to Indigenous and non-Indigenous students would provide all children with the same opportunities for success in terms of further education and/or employment. No acknowledgment was given to differing life experiences and backgrounds. Failure to recognize the extent to which ethnocentrism and racism permeate Canadian society continues to restrict necessary changes to school curricula.

For some Indigenous children, public schooling did serve as a key to progress. But for the vast majority, the culture shock and racist experiences—from the overt to microaggressions—that were first perpetrated in residential school continued in other forms in the public schools. Students frequently found themselves in classrooms with white middle-class teachers who had little to no understanding of their students' life circumstances, Indigenous knowledges, or the skills needed to cross the socio-cultural boundaries between themselves and their Indigenous students. Curricula that focused on Euro-Canadian issues and that belittled or more frequently ignored First People's persisting presence on the lands that became Canada did little to enhance Indigenous students' self-esteem or their desire for knowledge. A substitute teacher tells of an Indigenous student working on a history project in the hallway of a public elementary school. She was to research nineteenth-century modes of transportation using the *World Book Encyclopedia*'s entries on steam engines. When he questioned her about her grandparents, she demonstrated her knowledge of nineteenth-century Indigenous modes of transportation on the Northwest coast. But this was not part of the recognized curriculum and consequently was not given attention in the classroom. In the words of Alvin and Bert McKay of the Nisga'a School District, "No attempt was ever made to involve the people of the Nass in the content of the school courses. Instead, teachers, curriculum guides, texts, and materials were brought in" (McKay and McKay 1987, 71).

THE 1970S: "INDIAN CONTROL OF INDIAN EDUCATION" (NATIONAL INDIAN BROTHERHOOD 1972)

Years ago, the National Indian Brotherhood summed up its concerns in this way: "It has been the Indian student who was asked to integrate: to give up his identity, to adopt new values and a new way of life" (25–26) Even on the playground, Indigenous children faced (and continue to face) hostility and outright racism. The National Indian Brotherhood's policy statement, "Indian Control of Indian Education," from which that comment was taken, served as a major turning point in First Nations education in Canada. Issued partly as a response to an unacceptable white paper circulated by the Department of Indian Affairs, it emphasized the significance of local control and parental involvement in Indigenous children's education. One of the authors stated in a later paper,

> Our aim is to affect a true sense of identity for ourselves by recognizing traditional values while simultaneously preparing ourselves to function effectively in the larger society. (Kirkness 1978, 80)

Although some culturally relevant classrooms and programs existed prior to the Brotherhood's policy paper, it served to focus the attention of both governments and Indigenous people themselves on some issues of fundamental importance to Indigenous students. It remains a landmark document that sadly has ongoing relevance in 2022.[12]

Closely following the Indian control statement, in the late seventies, statistics showing Indigenous students' lack of success in public schools began to surface with regularity. The 94 percent school-leaving rate for First Nations students between kindergarten and grade 12 was constantly quoted (Hawthorn 1967, 130). At the same time, people recognized that a lack of positive role models in schools was proving detrimental to Indigenous students. Consequently, within the province, Indigenous groups such as the BC Native Indian Teachers' Association and established educational institutions worked to develop programs designed to encourage Indigenous people to consider teaching as a career. One such program is the previously mentioned Native Indian Teacher Education Program, started in 1974 at the University of British Columbia. The proposal for the program pointed out that there were at that time twenty-four Indigenous teachers in the province. If Indigenous teachers were represented in proportion to the general population, there should have been 1,300.

Throughout the seventies, Indigenous parents began to intervene more directly in their children's education; teachers and school boards could no longer dismiss them. Indigenous education committees made up of concerned parents and politicians formed in communities and in school districts. Home-school coordinators

12 See the original document at https://oneca.com/IndianControlofIndianEducation.pdf.

served as official links between the community and the school. In Williams Lake, Secwépemc educator and community member Phyllis Chelsea ran for the local school board and was elected. In northern BC in 1974, the Nisga'a established the first First Nations school district in the province. Indigenous language programs, often taught by community members, began on reserves and in public schools. In one situation, a parent who expressed interest in a language program for a federal school was recruited by the regular teacher and the following Monday began what became a seven-year teaching stint. Funded by the Special Education Branch of BC's provincial education department, coordinators of Indigenous education, Indigenous students' counsellors, and Indigenous teacher's aides began work in schools and districts with significant Indigenous student populations.

THE 1980S: COMMUNITY SCHOOLS

Most of the foregoing reforms were implemented within pre-existing educational systems—either the federally operated DIA schools or within the provincially funded and administered public schools. In the eighties, a new form of school emerged. The subject of long discussion, community-run schools were a significant change from the earlier forms of schooling available to Indigenous students. Although they depended for the most part on federal funds, the actual administration of the schools, including hiring practices and curricular choices, became the responsibility of the nation concerned. Opting to move outside existing systems in order to make real changes to the control of their children's schooling, the members of these communities took on a major task. Mount Currie,

Alkali Lake, Canim Lake, and Bella Coola were some of the original First Nation communities in BC that followed this route.

In 1983, there were 183 First Nation–controlled schools in Canada compared to 170 federal schools, and 16 percent of the First Nations students in Canada were attending the community-based schools (Canadian Education Association 1984, 13–14). In 1984, there were 187 schools enrolling 23 percent of First Nations students (Barman et al. 1986, 7). In BC, hiring flexibility was one of the attractions. Although Indigenous teachers with full provincial qualifications were hired as classroom teachers, one community hired an "unqualified" principal. His history with and understanding of the community was deemed far more important than a university degree to keeping the school meaningful and successful for both children and their parents.

The Department of Indian Affairs continued to control the dollars for First Nations education throughout the country. In BC, the Master Tuition Agreement remained the subject of much discontent. It enabled the federal and provincial governments and local school districts to negotiate money earmarked for First Nations students with no involvement of First Nations people themselves. Some of that funding was diverted into the general coffers of public schools with the claim that what benefited all students—such as a new gymnasium—would also benefit the Indigenous students. That agreement was suspended in 1986. Drawing on the criticisms of the bipartite agreement and following years of development, a new tripartite agreement was signed in 2018, replacing the original: Supporting First Nation Student Success allowed equal input from the First Nations of the province.[13]

13 See the original 2018 document here: http://www.fnesc.ca/wp/wp-content/uploads/2018/08/AGREEMENT-BCTEA-2018-FINAL-Signed-with-Schedules-WEB-VERSION-2018-08-1.pdf

INDIGENOUS CONTROL OF ADULT EDUCATION

Because of schools' general lack of success with Indigenous students, adult education programs became particularly important. Many who were pushed out of school without graduating chose to return to formal schooling as adults. While adult education programs had been in operation for decades, there were clear moves by Indigenous people to increase their influence in this sphere as well. The programs specifically for Indigenous adults varied from upgrading to vocational training and university courses such as teacher education and law. A focus on science and health careers soon followed.

As with schooling for children, the institutions and organizations that offered programs for adults followed one of two routes. Some reformers chose to operate within existing institutions. Others in search of more radical change chose to establish programs outside the control of the dominant society. There were, of course, advantages and disadvantages to both. Reform may have significant effects for the entire existing institution. As adaptations are made to include Indigenous students, the institution itself is changed. On the other hand, working in an independently controlled institution allows for greater variation in and respect for Indigenous approaches and more flexibility in addressing Indigenous knowledges and specific student needs. A major disadvantage of some independent institutions is that, although the education offered may be sound and more effective, other established institutions may refuse to recognize courses or give credit for them to students who want to continue their studies in those institutions. And funding remains an issue for all post-secondary institutions.

Within BC's provincially recognized institutions, the college preparation course offered by Fraser Valley College (now University of the Fraser Valley) in Chilliwack became a program that appealed to Indigenous students and made specific attempts to address their needs while preparing them for success in future college work. NITEP and the Native Law program, both offered by UBC, worked to combine the best of both worlds: relevant curriculum and support systems as needed, with all the regular requirements of a degree program. The Native Education Centre in Vancouver, which affiliated with Vancouver Community College in the '80s, operated relatively independently. Run by a non-profit society consisting of an Indigenous board and staffed predominantly by Indigenous people, the centre offered programs from Indigenous business management to upgrading, computer programming, and college preparation. While building on the strengths of the Indigenous students who came there, the staff also recognized that students might want to continue their education at other non-Indigenous institutions and structured their courses of study accordingly. Now the Native Education College, the school continues its work with a range of adult education programs.[14]

In the Kamloops area, a number of Indigenous-controlled educational institutions offered programs to Indigenous adults. In 1986–1987, the Secwepemc Cultural Education Society offered an upgrading program purchased from Vancouver's Native Education Centre and a college preparation program. The Native Training Institute, operating out of nearby Spences Bridge, emphasized a life skills approach to formal learning. While offering courses labelled English, Sociology, and Psychology, the instructors emphasized

14 See https://www.necvancouver.org/.

student involvement, Indigenous perspectives, and Indigenous process along with content. Almost all staff were Indigenous. The Friendship Centre and the BC Native Women's Society also offered courses for special interest groups such as long-term unemployed Indigenous people who were seeking job skills. All these institutions worked with some understanding of the context of the students' home and community backgrounds. The students' experiences with schooling could then provide a starting point for needed skill development in the area of choice. Indigenous administrators from several of these programs met on a regular basis to discuss the possibilities of establishing an Indigenous-controlled college in British Columbia.

A continuing concern of many Indigenous communities has been the limit to available funding for post-secondary students. As more adults return to school and move into post-secondary education, funding levels are failing to meet the increasing numbers. While some Indigenous people had joined the ranks of the Department of Indian Affairs and may have been trying to change the system from within, others felt that only a system that was locally based and that effectively addressed local concerns could improve the relationship of individual communities with the federal government and meet the real needs of the people.

References and Further Reading

"Acts of Visitation." 1943–1966. Kamloops Indian Residential School. Oblate Archives, Vancouver, BC.

Adams, David W. 1988. "Before Canada: Toward an Ethnohistory of Indian Education." *History of Education Quarterly.* Vol. 28, No. 1, Spring.

Angus, Mary, Ann Paul, and Karen Thomas. 1983. *The Summer Student Project: Ren Kyé7e (My Grandmother).* Kamloops: BC Native Women's Society.

Anonymous. 1908. Letter. Ottawa, March 21. PABC RG 10 Vol. 6001, File 1-1-1, Pt. 2, School Files.

Apple, Michael. 1979. *Ideology and Curriculum.* Boston: Routledge and Kegan Paul.

Apple, Michael. 1981. "Social Structure, Ideology and Curriculum." In *Rethinking Curriculum Studies,* edited by Martin Lawn and Len Barton. London: Croom Helm.

Archibald, Jo-ann. 1984. "Locally Developed Native Studies Curriculum: An Historical and Philosophical Rationale." Presented to the International Conference of the Mokakit Indian Education Research Association. London: University of Western Ontario.

Ashworth, Mary. 1979. *The Forces Which Shaped Them.* Vancouver: New Star Books.

Barman, Jean, Yvonne Hébert, and Don McCaskill, eds. 1986. *Indian Education in Canada, Volume 1: The Legacy.* Vancouver: University of British Columbia Press.

Barman, Jean, Yvonne Hébert, and Don McCaskill, eds. 1987. *Indian Education in Canada, Volume 2: The Challenge.* Vancouver: University of British Columbia Press.

Battiste, Marie. 1986. "Micmac Literacy and Cognitive Assimilation." In *Indian Education in Canada, Volume 1,* edited by Jean Barman et al. Vancouver: University of British Columbia Press.

Becker, Howard S. 1963. *Outsiders.* New York: The Free Press.

Becker, Howard S. 1970. *Sociological Work.* New Brunswick, NJ: Aldine Publishing Company.

Berger, Thomas. 1977. *Northern Frontier; Northern Homeland: The Report of the Mackenzie Valley Pipeline Inquiry. Volume 2, Terms and Conditions.* Ottawa: Ministry of Supply and Services Canada.

Berger, Thomas. 1981. *Fragile Freedoms.* Vancouver: Clarke, Irwin & Co.

Borg, Walter R., and Meredith D. Gall. 1979. *Educational Research.* New York: Longman.

Bowd, Alan D. 1977. "Ten Years after the Hawthorn Report." *Canadian Psychological Review.* Vol. 18, No. 4, October.

British Columbia and First Nations Education Steering Committee (FNESC). 2018. "BC Tripartite Education Agreement: Supporting First Nation Student Success." Accessed March 27, 2022. https://www2.gov.bc.ca/assets/gov/education/ways -to-learn/aboriginal-education/bc-tripartite-education-agreement.pdf.

British Columbia Royal Commission on Indian Affairs. 1913. Evidence submitted to the Royal Commission. Kamloops Agency.

Brody, Hugh. 1981. *Maps and Dreams.* Vancouver: Douglas & McIntyre.

Brow, Catherine Judith. 1967. "A Socio-cultural History of the Alkali Lake Shuswap, 1882–1966." Master's thesis. University of Washington.

Canada and the Plaintiffs. 2006. "Indian Residential Schools Settlement Agreement." Accessed March 27, 2022. https://www.residentialschoolsettlement.ca/IRS%20 Settlement%20Agreement-%20ENGLISH.pdf.

Canadian Education Association. 1984. *Recent Developments in Native Education.* Toronto.

Cardinal, Harold. 1977. *The Rebirth of Canada's Indians.* Edmonton: Hurtig Publishers.

Coates, Kenneth. 1985. "'Betwixt and Between': The Anglican Church and the Children of Carcross (Chooutla) Residential School, 1911–1954." *BC Studies.* Vol. 64, Winter.

Creighton, Donald. 1974. *Canada.* Toronto: Macmillan of Canada.

Cronin, Kay. 1960. *Cross in the Wilderness.* Vancouver: Mitchell Press.

Davin, Nicholas F. 1879. *Report on Industrial Schools for Indians and Half-Breeds.* Ottawa, March 14. PARC RG 10 Vol. 6001 File 1-1-1, Pt. 1.

Dawson, George M. 1891. *Notes on the Shuswap People of British Columbia.* Transactions of the Royal Society of Canada.

Department of Citizenship and Immigration, Indian Affairs Branch. 1960. *Indians of British Columbia (An Historical Review).* Ottawa: Indian Affairs Branch.

Duff, Wilson. 1964. *The Indian History of British Columbia.* Victoria: Provincial Museum of Natural History and Anthropology.

Fisher, Robin. 1977. *Contact and Conflict.* Vancouver: University of British Columbia Press.

Freire, Paulo. 1970. *Pedagogy of the Oppressed.* New York: Continuum.

Fulton, Hilary J.M. 1972. *The Melting Snowman.* Ottawa: Department of Indian Affairs and Northern Development.

Gamblin, Ronald. n.d. "Land Back! What Do We Mean?" 4Rs Youth Movement. Accessed March 27, 2022. https://4rsyouth.ca/land-back-what-do-we-mean.

Gibellini, Rosino, ed. 1979. *Frontiers of Theology in Latin America.* Maryknoll: Orbis Books.

Giroux, Henry A. 1981. *Ideology, Culture, and the Process of Schooling.* Philadelphia: Temple University Press.

Gooderham, Kent. 1972. *Notice: This Is an Indian Reserve.* Toronto: Griffin House.

Gooderham, Kent, ed. 1969. *I Am an Indian.* Toronto: J.M. Dent and Sons.

Grant, John Webster. 1984. *Moon of Wintertime.* Toronto: University of Toronto Press.

Gresko, Jacqueline (Kennedy). 1969. "Roman Catholic Missionary Effort and Indian Acculturation in the Fraser Valley, B.C. 1860–1900." Unpublished BA honours essay, University of British Columbia.

Gresko, Jacqueline (Kennedy). 1979. "White 'Rites' and Indian 'Rites': Indian Education and Native Responses in the West, 1870–1910." In *Shaping the Schools of the Canadian West,* edited by David C. Jones, Robert M. Stamp, and Nancy M. Sheehan. Calgary: Detselig.

Gresko, Jacqueline (Kennedy). 1986. "Creating Little Dominions within the Dominion: Early Catholic Indian Schools in Saskatchewan and British Columbia." In *Indian Education in Canada, Volume 1,* edited by Jean Barman et al. Vancouver: University of British Columbia Press.

Haig-Brown, Celia. 1988. *Resistance and Renewal: Surviving the Indian Residential School*. Vancouver: Tillicum Library, a division of Arsenal Pulp Press.

Hawthorn, H.B., ed. 1967. *A Survey of the Contemporary Indians of Canada, Vol. 11*. Ottawa: Queen's Printer.

Hewlett, Edward Sleigh. 1964. "The Chilcotin Uprising: A Study of Indian-White Relations in Nineteenth Century British Columbia." Master's thesis, University of British Columbia.

Hill-Tout, Charles. 1907. *British North America 1. The Far West*. London: Archibald Constable and Co.

Indian Act. 1978. Ottawa: Queen's Printer.

Indian Affairs Branch and University of British Columbia Extension Department. 1967. *Proceedings of the Conference on the Indian Child and His Education*. Vancouver: University of British Columbia Extension Department.

Indian Affairs Education Division. 1965. *The Education of Indian Children in Canada*. Toronto: Ryerson Press.

Ignace, Marianne, and Ronald E. Ignace. 2017. *Secwépmec People, Land, and Laws*. Montreal: McGill-Queen's University Press.

Jack, Agnes, ed. 2006. *Behind Closed Doors*. Penticton: Theytus Books.

Jack, Rita. 1985. "Legacy of the Indian Residential School." *Secwepemc Cultural Arts Magazine*. Vol. 1, No. 1.

Jenness, Diamond. 1963. *The Indians of Canada*. Ottawa: Information Canada.

Johnston, Basil H. 1988. *Indian School Days*. Toronto: Key Porter Press.

King, A. Richard. 1967. *The School at Mopass*. Toronto: Holt, Rinehart and Winston.

Kirk, Ruth. 1986. *Wisdom of the Elders*. Vancouver: Douglas & McIntyre in association with the BC Provincial Museum.

Kirkness, Verna J. 1978. *Evaluation Report of Indians in Federal and Provincial Schools in Manitoba*. Ottawa: Department of Indian Affairs and Northern Development.

Kirkness, Verna J. 1981. "The Education of Canadian Indian Children," *Child Welfare*. Vol. 60, No. 7, July–August.

Kirkness, Verna J. 1985. "Indian Teachers—A Key to Progress." Address to University of Saskatoon, February 27.

Kleinfeld, Judith. 1975. "Effective Teachers of Eskimo and Indian Students." *School Review.* Vol. 83, No. 2, February.

Latham, Barbara K., and Roberta J. Pazdro, eds. 1984. *Not Just Pin Money.* Victoria: Camosun College.

LaViolette, Forrest E. 1973. *The Struggle for Survival.* Toronto: University of Toronto Press.

MacLaurin, Donald. 1936. "The History of Education in the Crown Colonies of Vancouver Island and British Columbia and in the Province of British Columbia." PhD dissertation, University of Washington.

Maclean, John. 1896. *Canadian Savage Folk.* Toronto: William Briggs.

Mann, Peter H. 1968. *Methods of Social Investigation.* New York: Basil Blackwell Ltd.

Manuel, George, and Michael Posluns. 1974. *The Fourth World.* Toronto: Collier-Macmillan.

Matthew, Marie. 1986. *Introduction to the Shuswap People.* Kamloops: Secwepemc Cultural Education Society.

McKay, Alvin, and Bert McKay. 1987. "Education as a Total Way of Life: The Nisga'a Experience." In *Indian Education in Canada, Volume 2,* edited by Jean Barman et al. Vancouver: University of British Columbia Press.

Merkel, Ray H. n.d. "Traditional Indian Education." Unpublished paper of the Traditional Indian Education Society.

Miller, Kahn-Tineta, George Lerchs, and Robert G. Moore. 1978. *The Historical Development of the Indian Act.* Edited by John Leslie and Ron Maguire. Ottawa[?]: Treaties and Historical Research Centre, P.R.E. Group, Indian and Northern Affairs, August.

Monture-Angus, Patricia. 1995. *Thunder in My Soul.* Nova Scotia: Fernwood Publishing.

Monture-Angus, Patricia. 1998. "Standing against Canadian Law: Naming Omissions of Race, Culture and Gender." *New Zealand Yearbook of New Zealand Jurisprudence.* Vol. 2. http://www.nzlii.org/nz/journals/NZYbkNZJur/1998/2.html.

More, Arthur J. 1978. Unpublished paper, University of British Columbia.

More, Arthur J. 1984. *Okanagan Nicola Indian Quality of Education Study.* Penticton: Okanagan Indian Learning Institute.

Morice, A.G. [1906] 1978. *The History of the Northern Interior of British Columbia.* Smithers: Interior Stationery.

Morse, J.J. 1949. "Education Comes to Kamloops." *Kamloops Sentinel*, July 11.

Mulvihill, James. 1957. "On Integration." Tape 130-2. Kamloops: Secwepemc Cultural Education Society Resource Centre.

National Indian Brotherhood. 1972. "Indian Control of Indian Education." Policy paper presented to the Minister of Indian Affairs and Northern Development. Ottawa: National Indian Brotherhood/Assembly of First Nations. Accessed March 27, 2022. https://oneca.com/IndianControlofIndianEducation.pdf.

Ormsby, Margaret A. 1958. *British Columbia*. Toronto: Macmillan.

Parminter, Alfred Vye. 1964. "The Development of Integrated Schooling for British Columbia Indian Children." Master's thesis, University of British Columbia.

Persson, Diane. 1980. "Blue Quills: A Case Study of Indian Residential Schooling." PhD dissertation, University of Alberta.

Persson, Diane. 1986. "The Changing Experience of Indian Residential Schooling: Blue Quills, 1913–1970." In *Indian Education in Canada, Volume 1*, edited by Jean Barman et al. Vancouver: University of British Columbia Press.

Peterson, Lester Ray. 1959. "Indian Education in British Columbia." Master's thesis, University of British Columbia.

Polakow, Valerie. 1985. "Whose Stories Should We Tell? A Call to Action." *Language Arts*. Vol. 62, No. 8, December.

Prentice, Alison L., and Susan E. Houston, eds. 1975. *Family, School & Society in Nineteenth-Century Canada*. Toronto: Oxford University Press.

Quade, Quentin L., ed. 1982. *The Pope and Revolution*. Washington, DC: Ethics and Public Policy Center.

Redford, James. 1979–1980. "Attendance at Indian Residential Schools In British Columbia, 1890–1920." *BC Studies*. No. 44, Winter.

Secwepemc Cultural Arts Magazine. 1985. Vol. 1, No. 1, June.

Secwepemc Cultural Education Society. 1977. "Kamloops Indian Residential School." *Kamloops Souvenir Edition*, May 21.

Secwepemc Cultural Education Society. 1982. *The Shuswap Declaration*. Kamloops: Secwepemc Cultural Education Society.

Sellars, Bev. 2013. *They Called Me Number One*. Vancouver: Talonbooks.

Special Joint Committee of the Senate and the House of Commons Appointed to Examine and Consider the Indian Act. 1947. *Minutes of Proceedings and Evidence*, No. 1. Ottawa: King's Printer.

St. Onge, L.N. 1892. *Letter to Father Lejeune*. Troy, New York. Kamloops: SCES Vertical File: Father Lejeune.

Stanbury, W.T. 1975. *Success and Failure*. Vancouver: University of British Columbia Press.

Sterling, Shirley. 1992. *My Name Is Seepeetza*. Toronto: Groundwood Books.

Supreme Court of Canada. 1997. Supreme Court Judgments. *Delgamuukw v. British Columbia*. December 11. https://scc-csc.lexum.com/scc-csc/scc-csc/en/item/1569/index.do.

Teit, James. [1900] 1975. *The Thompson Indians of British Columbia*. New York: AMS Press.

Teit, James. [1909] 1975. *The Shuswap*. New York: AMS Press.

Titley, E. Brian. 1984. "Duncan Campbell Scott and Indian Education Policy." In *An Imperfect Past*, edited by J. Donald Wilson. Vancouver: University of British Columbia CSCI.

Titley, E. Brian. 1986. *A Narrow Vision*. Vancouver: University of British Columbia Press.

Union of British Columbia Indian Chiefs. 1971. *Claims Based on Native Title*. Vancouver: Union of British Columbia Indian Chiefs.

University of British Columbia. n.d. "NITEP. The Indigenous Teacher Education Program." Accessed March 27, 2022. https://nitep.educ.ubc.ca.

Vankoughnet, Lawrence. 1887. *Letter to John A. MacDonald*. Ottawa, August 26. PABC RG 10 Vol. 6001 File 1-1-1, Pt. 1.

Vayro, Celia Haig-Brown. 1986. "Invasion and Resistance: Native Perspectives of the Kamloops Indian Residential School." Master's thesis, University of British Columbia.

Vizenor, Gerald. 1999. *Manifest Manners*. Lincoln: University of Nebraska Press.

Vizenor, Gerald. 2008. "Aesthetics of Survivance: Literary Theory and Practice." In *Survivance*, edited by Gerald Vizenor. Lincoln: University of Nebraska Press.

Wax, Murray L., Rosalie H. Wax, and Robert V. Dumont Jr. 1964. *Formal Education in an American Indian Community*. Kalamazoo: The Society for the Study of Social Problems.

Werner, Walter, et al. 1977. *Whose Culture? Whose Heritage?* Vancouver: University of British Columbia Centre for Curriculum and Instruction.

Whitehead, Margaret. 1981. *The Cariboo Mission.* Victoria: Sono Nis Press.

Whyte, William Foote. 1955. *Street Corner Society.* Chicago: University of Chicago Press.

Willis, Paul. 1977. *Learning to Labour.* New York: Columbia University Press.

Wilson, J. Donald. 1986. "'No Blanket to Be Worn in School': The Education of Indians in Nineteenth Century Ontario." In *Indian Education in Canada, Volume 1*, edited by Jean Barman et al. Vancouver: University of British Columbia Press.

Wilson, J. Donald, and David C. Jones, eds. 1980. *Schooling and Society in 20th Century British Columbia.* Calgary: Detselig Enterprises Ltd.

Witvliet, Theo. 1985. *A Place in the Sun Liberation.* London: SCM Press.

Wolcott, Harry F. 1967. *A Kwakiutl Village and School.* Toronto: Holt, Rinehart and Winston.

RELEVANT WEBSITES

CBC. "48 Books by Indigenous Writers to Read to Understand Residential Schools." Curated by David A. Robertson. https://www.cbc.ca/books/48-books-by -indigenous-writers-to-read-to-understand-residential-schools-1.6056204.

Indian Residential School Survivors Society. https://www.irsss.ca/.

Indian Residential School Survivors Society Crisis Line. https://www.irsss.ca/faqs/ how-do-i-reach-the-24-hour-crisis-line.

National Centre for Truth and Reconciliation. "Reports." https://nctr.ca/records/ reports/#nctr-reports.

Native Education College. https://www.necvancouver.org/.

Sk'elep School of Excellence. https://skelep.com.

Tk'emlúps te Sewépemc. "Language and Culture Department." https://tkemlups.ca/ profile/history/our-language.

Tk'emlúps te Sewépemc. "Sk'elep School of Excellence." https://tkemlups.ca/ departments/education/skelep-school-excellence.

Index

Note: Page numbers in italics indicate a photograph.

Photo credit: Lindsay Swanson

CELIA HAIG-BROWN is an educator now based in Ontario. Her book *Resistance and Renewal: Surviving the Indian Residential School* (upon which *Tsqelmucwílc* is based) was published in 1988 by Tillicum Library (an imprint of Arsenal Pulp Press) and won the Roderick Haig-Brown Regional Prize. Her other books include *Taking Control: Power and Contradiction in First Nations Adult Education* and *With Good Intentions: Euro-Canadian and Aboriginal Relations in Colonial Canada* (both UBC Press). Recently, she has turned to documentary film, and her work has been shown at the Smithsonian's Native American Film + Video Festival in New York and the Irvine International Film Festival in California.

GARRY GOTTFRIEDSON is a Secwépemc poet with ten books to his credit. In 1987, he attended the Naropa Institute in Boulder, Colorado, where he studied creative writing under such instructors as Allen Ginsberg and Marianne Faithfull. Currently he is the Secwépemc Cultural Advisor to Thompson Rivers University.

RANDY FRED is an Elder of Tseshaht First Nation who survived nine years at the Alberni Indian Residential School. After a lifelong career in multimedia, he is currently the Nuu-Chah-Nulth Elder at Vancouver Island University.